PRANAY PATIL

BURGUNDY WINTERS
in Europe

Crystal Peake Publisher
www.crystalpeake.co.uk

First edition published in 2022 by Crystal Peake Publisher

Hardback 978-1-912948-41-3
Mass Market Print 978-1-912948-44-4
Trade Print 978-1-912948-43-7
eBook 978-1-912948-42-0

Text copyright © Pranay Patil 2022
Cover © Pete Heyes 2022

All rights reserved. No part of this publication may be reproduced, stored in or introduced into a retrieval system, or transmitted, in any form, or by any means (electrical, mechanical, photocopying, recording or otherwise) without the prior written permission of the publisher. Any person who does any unauthorised act in relation to this publication may be liable to criminal prosecution and civil claims for damages.

A catalogue copy of this book is available from the British Library.
Published in England, United Knigdom.

Typeset by Crystal Peake Publisher
Cover illustrations by Pete Heyes
Edited by Nicola Peake Editing
About the author by Maddy, New York
Foreword by Ms. Alexandria, Germany
Introduction by Pranay Patil
Photography by Emma Charlotte.
News partner - The Honest Herald, Defenders of Unpopular Truth
Radio partner - Wylin'5 FM, Manhattan's #1 Campus Station
Charity arm - Honest Foundation, New York & Abhaji Kisan Sena-A Farmers' Union, India

Visit www.crystalpeake.co.uk for any further information.

BURGUNDY WINTERS
in Europe

PRANAY PATIL

"To love, guilt, abuse and the occult… and to all the lives Peruvian-Albin has destroyed."

Reviews are the most powerful tools for a publisher and an author, they help to gain attention for the books you enjoy reading. Honest reviews of our books help to bring them to the attention of other readers.

If you have enjoyed this book or any of our other books we would be very grateful if you could spend just five minutes leaving a review. These reviews can be as short or as long as you like.

Contents

Foreword	11
About The Author	13
Acknowledgments	15
Introduction	17
Chapter One	21
Chapter Two	67
Chapter Three	111
Chapter Four	157
Chapter Five	201
Chapter Six	245
Chapter Seven	289

Foreword

By Ms. Alexandria, Germany

Trying to take on a whole continent in 15 days might seem a little far-fetched, but Pranay Patil shows that it is indeed possible! He was able to take me on a tour through some wonderful places in Europe, giving me insight and historical facts, without making it seem like reading a travel guide.

Jace and Yasmine came alive through Patil's charming words and his gift to unite romance, history and adventure. They meet in Paris, and after a few turbulent weeks, start their trip through some of the most popular tourist sites of Europe.

It would have been easy for Patil to stay in the shallow waters of a simple romance story and to show Jace and Yasmine wandering around pretty sites exchanging flowery words, but Patil doesn't stop there. He shows a depth to his characters that speaks to his capabilities as a writer. And while Jace and Yasmine are touring Europe, they explore the hidden corners of their hearts. Because both have been through traumatic experiences in the past, moving forward and letting go of those ghosts seems difficult and almost impossible. Oh and some of those ghosts… they're not figuratively at all. Jace and Yasmine are actually chased by ghosts that attack them all across Europe!

It is an intriguing story to read, because of mysterious

ghosts not withstanding the people in this book seem real. They have problems and character flaws; they make mistakes and learn to own up to them, but most of all they learn that love comes in many forms: forgiveness, support and trust.

About The Author

Pranay Patil is a dreamer, engineer, foodie, and social activist living in rural India, helping the underserved get justice. In between studying engineering in Germany, Pranay began travelling extensively around Europe. While sharing stories of his adventures with his friends, he realised these vivid experiences needed to make their way on to paper. This is how his first novel, Burgundy Winters, was born.

100% of his book sale profits go towards charity organisations, helping children from marginalised sections of society get quality education.

When he's not writing, you'll find Pranay harvesting fresh produce from his farms to cook up culinary masterpieces.

Acknowledgments

Payal, Laura, Riley and Cole.

Introduction

By Pranay Patil

Life is sacred. It is a beautiful gift of time, experience, and love, but is terrifyingly fragile. As we live our lives, it is so easy to coast and not enjoy the precious time we have on earth. Time flies when you're having fun, but also when you're not paying attention. One moment you're a bright-eyed college graduate entering the workforce, and the next you're attending a retirement party with your name on the cake. In the blink of an eye, your prime days can pass without warning.

People have their own unique ways of enjoying their spare time. Most people live for the weekend, grinding away at their 9-5 job until Friday night. This cycle repeats over and over, becoming a cruel habit. Repetition breeds mindlessness, which only encourages the clock to tick faster. Yet much of the population has no other option, so they instead opt to maximise their spare time. Some people spend it at the bar, others in the outdoors, or spending time with family.

Instead of physical experience, a growing percentage of the population is opting for a different type of escape: psychological trips. Recreational drugs, once enjoyed by or reserved for either rockstars or junkies, are quickly catching on in the general population. With the legalisation and regulation of marijuana in many regions, recreational drugs are also becoming safer. Yet people still want more. They go for the harder drugs, that produce an amplified experience that alters their mind and reality. Venturing outside of the regulation can create incredible experiences, but can also breed addiction, overdose, and a trip in a hearse.

Often, all we need is a wake-up call to realise the dangerous lifestyles we lead. The morbidity of death is the most common type of shock. When someone very close to us is taken away, it creates a well of many emotions. Of course sadness, but also regret for not making the most of our time together on earth. For some people, it can also bring guilt. While death is a natural part of life, it is easy to feel guilt for not stopping it.

These wake-up calls are life-changing, but they are also necessary. They require us to take a hard look at our lives and the dangerous choices we make. Often, loss can be exactly what we need to change our lives for the best. But this realisation doesn't come easy. It is difficult to forgive ourselves when death is, in our minds, on our hands. It is a process, not an overnight fix. Therapy, rehab, and professional help is a great option. In Burgundy Winters, Jace finds self-forgiveness through a French tour guide, Yasmine.

Forgiving oneself is the final piece to the puzzle following loss. There is a time for mourning, but changes need to be made to break the cycle. This book follows the journey of two young individuals as they break away from their destructive habits and find forgiveness, understanding, and even love. Burgundy Winters is not a glamorous and fluffy romance novel, but instead an inspiring tale of overcoming addiction and abuse and finding real beauty in a cold world.

Lots of love,

Pranay Patil.

Chapter One
Jace Tanner

Excitement, euphoria, and elation are the emotions I hold at this very moment. I feel so thrilled to be here. The comfort of being with my best buddy and lead vocalist, Aiden Gill, our bassist Russ, and drummer Cross, seems so illusory. At times, I have to remind myself that all of it's real.

Our band, Soft Division, started a few years ago, and I'm the lead guitarist. It all seemed like a joke when we blew up a few seasons ago. Our original two albums made it to the international Billboard charts. Since then, our lives have turned. All four of ours.

The raging crowd draws me back to the real world, and I dance around the stage. I connect with my bandmates as we play, not enough to wreck the music, of course, but just enough for one to see that we love rock and enjoy performing for a living. I lose the ability to breathe for a moment as the rhythm plays and the crowd chants. My spirit soars after realising how much the audience admires our music. Throughout the night, the entire audience continues to hum with us and move along to the rhythm.

'Praise you all!' The four of us yell at the top of our voices as we round up; the crowd goes insane as we get off the stage.

'That was crazy!' Aiden exclaims.

I guess I'm not the only one happy here. Russ and Cross also look thrilled.

'Guys! I'm so proud of the four of you.' My sister Pearl, who doubles as our manager, catches us off guard and hugs us one after another.

Pearl is the reason we took this music thing seriously. She constantly encouraged us to chase our dreams. I love Pearl more than I care for my existence. Some see her as peculiar because she is into girls, but I say screw that! Love is devotion. Yes, my sister is a lesbian, and I admire her to death.

'Did you see that?' She hops in glee. 'How about we go to Darla's yacht tonight to celebrate?' she suggests.

However, we dismiss that offer almost instantly because we have other plans.

'We have stuff to do, Pearl, and that yacht is practically a monastery,' Aiden speaks first.

'That's vile, Aiden! Darla is such a charming young woman. You know what, guys? I'll spare you tonight. Tomorrow, we will have a nice breakfast. All five of us,' she declares, then strides away before we can resist. Typical Pearl, she knows how to coax us into accomplishing her ends.

Aiden picks up a bottle of Hennessy on the dresser next to him and takes a generous swig, then hands it over to me. I quaff it down before passing it to Cross, who gives it to Russ.

'Crazy how our two albums have been on the top spot

back-to-back, week after week. I'm super pleased,' Aiden comments.

'It wouldn't have been imaginable without you guys. All of you,' Russ replies with a massive grin plastered on his face. I merely bow as I continue sipping from the bottle that Aiden passed to me repeatedly.

'We should get moving. I need to get high on Peruvian-Albin,' I slur, already feeling tipsy.

The journey to the parking lot feels long as we try to avoid paparazzi and crazy fans who want to rip our clothes off. Finally, our limousine rolls to a halt in front of us; we lumber on our feet as we toil to get in. Being the life of the party, Aiden immediately turns on blaring music and starts bobbing his head to the beat as the ride begins.

'I don't think I can wait long enough for us to arrive at the hotel,' Russ says as he rolls himself a blunt.

'Never say never!' I say with a grin, pulling out my stash of Peruvian-Albin.

'You had Peruvian-Albin here, and no one noticed?' Aiden says, pretending to act annoyed.

'Let's do it.' Cross rubs his palms together and licks his lower lip. Trust Cross to be the eager one when he sees Peruvian-Albin. I roll up a dollar bill I found in my jeans pocket, then pouring Peruvian-Albin on the little table in front of me, I use the bill to sniff it in one go. Aiden, Russ, and Cross do the same, and before we know it, we're plastered.

Pearl was livid. 'I was busy last night, and I got a call that you guys kept on constituting nuisance at the reception. Do you realise how awful and embarrassing it was? Do you even know how you got into this bed, Jace?'

She kept on rambling about how I should be responsible. Pearl kept on talking about how all four of us are crackheads, and she expects more from me.

Trust Pearl to always act like she is the boss of everybody, I think to myself, growing annoyed by her constant meddles.

Speaking of everybody, I phoned them all to check if they knew how they got into bed. Unfortunately, none of us had a hint of how we were fitfully tucked in. The trip had already hammered us. We laugh about it and plan on definitely getting high again today.

'If you love your balls, you better not miss breakfast,' Aiden reminds me before he hangs up. The thought of Pearl getting annoyed again frightens me, so I freshen up.

I throw on a simple tapered white shirt and roll the sleeves up in a tight geometric precision with black trousers. As I put my hands in my pockets, I feel something inside. I yank it out, and see it's a blue pill, my favourite. I pop it almost immediately.

'Time to fly,' I say to myself, running my fingers through my blonde mane.

On arriving at the joint, I meet Aiden, Russ, and Cross talking to Pearl. It looks like she had been scolding them as she did to me.

'Sit,' she says, and I do as she directs. I casually greet my three allies at the table. 'Acting like fucking kids,' she groans under her breath before sitting up and reading the menu. 'I wouldn't hesitate to knock you guys out if I got any news that you four were on drugs again!' she warns.

Oh, Pearl, if only she knew.

The server arrives to take our order; we hang for a bit. The silence is awkward. It's slaying me, and nobody dares to utter a word because we all know it would piss Pearl off. Finally, our food arrives, and I brace to dig in.

'Oh my God, guys! Is that Soft Division?' A girl squeals, with her friend right beside her.

'Here we go again,' I murmur under my breath, but loud enough for Aiden to hear. He chuckles lowly.

She drags her friend to our table.

'Hi, Jace! Hi, Cross! Hi, Aiden! Hi, Russ!' she greets. One would suspect she knew all four of us privately. 'Oh, my God! This is like a dream come true,' she whisper-shrieks. 'My name is Lina, and I'm a tremendous fan. I would love to have a photograph or two with you guys,' she announces with a fat grin pasted on her face. You could see how elated she was.

'Uh, sure, why not, Lina?' Aiden answers and flashes them a smile, the killer smile, as we call it. We rise, and Lina brings out a small digital camera from her handbag and passes it to Pearl to take the picture.

'Big smile, gentlemen! Big smile!' she says before we hear a "click" sound indicating Pearl has taken the picture.

Pearl returns the camera, and Lina mouths a thank you to her. She rechecks the pictures and squeals.

'Oh, my God! They look so cute!' Lina exclaims. 'Thank you, Soft Division. I hope I get to see you guys again,' she says and surges back to her table with excitement while her friend follows suit.

'Well, that was something,' Aiden sighs, and I kick him from underneath the table. We both laugh, and everybody eats.

After eating, Russ and Cross excuse themselves for some unfinished business, so now it's just Aiden, Pearl, and me at breakfast.

'I care for you guys. I love you guys so much and admire how you are doing the things you love, but please don't shatter your success with drugs.' Pearl sounded like she was going to break down.

'All right, Pearl. I promise we will try our best,' Aiden says and hugs her. She throws a modest smile that melts my heart. At least she is less upset than before.

She fixes her dress before standing up.

'I have to take off now. I have some business to attend to,' Pearl says. 'Bill, please,' she claps.

The waiter rushes down to our table with the bill in his hands, which Pearl pays off with her card. I would have loved to settle up, but I quit asking a long time ago because I knew she would decline it.

'All right boys, catch you later.' Pearl struts out of the joint in style.

'I feel awful,' Aiden speaks first.

'Why?' I ask

'I just bluffed to Pearl,' he says, suddenly letting out a quick grin. 'I love how she acts like a mum even if it's aggravating,' he purses his rims. 'I can't quit. That is the only thing that gets me there! The incredible sensation of heightened senses when I'm on Peruvian-Albin or meth or Canadian loud is irreplaceable. I'm like a cat in a strange garret when not on crack. Mmmh, the feeling is incomprehensible. Time flies when I'm high. It makes me feel the rush from the crowd during our performances,' he expresses with warmth in his peepers.

'I'll not bluff. I go through the same sensory hallucinations. How about we head back to your suite and smoke up?' I suggest.

'Of course, but of course! Let me call Russ and Cross

to meet us there,' Aiden says eagerly.

We both rise and head into Aiden's room.

'Boys!' I hear Cross' voice. He and Russ barge into the room.

They meet us in the cramped kitchen, with me sitting on the counter with an urn of beer in my grip and Aiden with a blunt. Aiden gives Russ his blunt. My best friend was looking hammered. He increases the speaker's sound to the highest volume. We dance around, each one of us extremely high.

'Hey, come snort this,' Russ tells Aiden.

A hard knock on the door echoes through the foyer. We scorn at it first, but the person bangs again. This time, I careen to the door and fling it open. A short man stands in the doorway. He seems to be in his early forties and is wearing an expensive-looking suit and a forlorn expression on his face. He looks somewhat familiar, and I try hard to remember his name before realising that I'm not immune to lethologica.

'Mr. Tanner?' he says, his voice ringing in my ear as I stand at his front. 'I believe we have met. I'm Donny, the manager of this hotel,' he pauses. 'I would rather get straight to the point, Mr. Tanner. We have received complaints from other customers that this suite has been loud, disrupting the peace of other guests. I'm afraid I'll have to ask you and your bunch to check out,' he states.

'Check out? What do you mean check out?' I yell at him.

'No need to yell, Mr Tanner. We will give you until midnight to check out,' the manager retorts.

What could be more humiliating? A mere manager being rude to me! Jace Tanner! I thrust him aside and clutched his collar. 'You don't fucking talk to me like that, Donny!' I yell.

'I... I...' he stammers and steps back, 'this is physical harassment, Mr Tanner. You still have until midnight to check out, else there will be repercussions,' he warns and storms out.

I slam the door shut and head to the kitchen, only to see my friends already high. Aiden is sleeping on the stool. Russ is relaxing on the counter, and Cross is sitting on the tiny living room settee. I shake my head in disgust, still pissed off at my encounter with the hotel manager.

'Jace!'

Pearl's voice echoes from my sleep. My eyes gently open; instincts don't lie. 'Ugh!' I whine and then sit up. Although the other three are nowhere in sight, I find myself still in Aiden's room.

'Did you harass Mr Donny?' Pearl asks, with her hands on her midriff. She looks like she is about to smack the hell out of me.

'He pissed me off, Pearl,' I whine like a child.

'Do you honestly think you can do anything because you are famous now, Jace? Where are your manners? Were you going to strike an older person because he advised you against disrupting the peace of other guests?' This time, Pearl was staring at me firmly. 'I don't think there is anything I can say anymore. I asked Aiden to go to your room and pack your bags. We leave in an hour. There is a hotel nearby; we will lodge there for three days and then return to Minnesota,' she takes one last glance at me, then leaves the room.

It has been three days since the episode at the hotel happened. Pearl has been dodging me for reasons I don't seem to grasp. However, today we're travelling back to Minnesota. Minnesota is where Aiden and I grew up. Our parents were tight friends until we lost them, and ever since then, Pearl became our guardian.

'I miss playing hockey. I can't wait to get back and whip your ass,' Aiden jokes as he pulls off his sweatpants.

He flings one of my shirts at me, but something falls from it. I bend to pick it up and see a stash of Peruvian-Albin.

'Should we be doing this?' Aiden asks before he snorts the last line of Peruvian-Albin on the table. 'That is the last one. We're never doing this again,' Aiden says, feeling guilty already. He dusts his nose with a paper towel, and I do the same.

'What do you think about a concert in Minnesota?' Aiden asks me.

I hoist my head to answer him, but suddenly I notice that his red and puffy eyes are swollen more than usual.

'Buddy, are you okay?' I ask, patting his shoulders, but before he can respond, he starts to cough nonstop. I scramble to the kitchen to grab him a cup of water. 'Here. Sip some water,' I suggest, but the cough persists.

Aiden coughs out blood. This time I get spooked and struggle to stop his persistent cough by forcing water into his mouth. The coughing does not stop; it's turning into a bark now. I cry for help, but nobody answers. I carry Aiden down to the car and zoom to the nearest hospital. As soon as we get out of the car, paramedics place Aiden on a stretcher and wheel him to the ER. I walk to the reception and park there for hours, waiting for the doctor to give me news. After I phone Cross to notify him of the situation at hand, I try to call Pearl, but it keeps going to her voicemail. Perhaps she is still pissed at me. A thought crosses my mind abruptly. I use Aiden's phone to call her, and she answers her phone. I explain the entire story to her, and she assures me she will be in the emergency room in an instant.

'Hello, Mr Tanner,' a youthful guy with a surgical mask taps my left shoulder. 'The doctor has sought an audience with you.'

'Me? Where is his office?' I inquire, squirming.

I head to the physician's room.

'Sit, Mr Tanner,' the doctor says. 'I'm afraid we lost your friend Aiden,' he says

I let out a short laugh because it sounded like a joke. 'You are joking, aren't you?'

I immediately barge out of the room and run to Aiden's ward. I see him there, lying stiff. His lips are blue, the colour of death. I shudder as I inch closer to him.

'Aiden,' I call softly at first. 'Doc says you have flatlined. How is that even possible? It's my fault, Aiden. All mine. Please, get up.'

His spirit of life was stolen by the frigid embrace of death. There was no flicker of existence. I continue staring at him and hope he will rise and reveal how he and the doctor were trying to prank me, thinking he will wake up and pull me into a tight hug, because that is what I need right now. I feel my eyes moisten and my vision blur.

My phone rings, and it's Pearl. She asks me to come to the front desk; I walk there with thoughts of how to break the news running through my mind.

'How is he?' Pearl's voice interrupts my thoughts.

'He... He... Aiden's gone, Pearl,' I stutter. Tears pour down from my eyes.

'If this is another one of your gags, Jace, you'd better quit it,' she says shakily. 'What happened? Where is he?'

Pearl asks multiple questions. She seems as rattled as

me. She follows me to his ward and pauses in her tracks as soon as she spots Aiden on the bed.

'What happened to him?' she whispers, touching his lifeless body. 'Have you spoken to the physician?' She wipes away her tears.

'I walked out on him. I still don't know what to say or how to react...'

She moves out, and I tag at her back. We meet the same doctor I had spoken to earlier. He acknowledges our presence by excusing himself from the medic with whom he is talking.

'Mr Tanner,' he nods his head to me.

'Hello, Doctor. I'm Pearl Tanner, guardian to Jace and the deceased,' she tries to suck her tears while talking.

'Mr Gill suffered a case of acute internal bleeding induced by excessive consumption of cocaine,' he points out.

Pearl throws me an evil glance, and I can hardly look at her.

'Thank you, Doctor,' Pearl says, trudging back to a lifeless Aiden. 'I warned you, Jace!' she screeches at the top of her voice.

I simply bow my head as she utters strange words to me, realising she is correct, recognising that I deserve whatever punishment comes my way for the death of my best buddy. It aches to lose your best buddy to the harsh hands of death. He was my brother. We lost our parents around the same time. What makes it worse is that now I have also lost Aiden forever.

I stare at the grave where I buried my closest friend and light a blunt. The blunts I smoke are the only things keeping me sane. Russ and Cross are impossible to locate. Life has little meaning at this stage. I drop the white roses I picked up for him on his grave. The headstone had Aiden's name chiselled on it. *In loving memory of our son, brother, friend. Aiden Gill 1987-2007.* Those words alone let tears roll down my eyes painfully.

'Hey, bro, I don't know if you can hear me. I know I can feel you around me all the time. Aiden, I miss you dreadfully. It sounds absurd, but I wish we listened to Pearl. Life feels like an endless chasm without you, buddy. This desolate sensation is overpowering,' I say all these words with tears streaming over my lips.

I wipe off my salty sorrow with the sleeve of my shirt, take another peek at the grave, and shuffle back to my car. Once I am in the car, I speed back to the apartment I have been avoiding because of the memories it holds of Aiden and me. As I step in, I see that everything looks the same as when we left it. I sob as I fall flat on the couch in my living room. After picking up my blunt from the table, I light it and pull a drag. For just a moment, I feel free from all my demons and horrors, and eventually, peace sweeps over me. Slowly, my eyelids close and sleep finally draws me in before I finish my blunt.

It's been a few weeks, and the news about Soft Division has spread far and wide. Everybody knows about it, and Russ and Cross are still nowhere to be found. And myself? The only things keeping me sane are my addictions and my sister.

'These things will not help, Jace! Do you wish to get yourself killed?' Pearl says, pointing to my Peruvian-Albin and blunts on the short stand by my bedside.

While ignoring her and lighting my blunt, I feel each puff closing like a fatal noose around my neck. It reeks of death.

'Jace,' she calls softly. 'I thought therapy would be good for you,' she repeats.

'You don't get to decide what I'm going to do with my life all the time, Pearl,' I snap at her.

'Yes, I do, Jace. I get to choose what you do with your life, since you are remarkably naïve to think for yourself. I let you decide for yourself before, but not anymore. Not after you and Aiden destroyed his life. I'll not let you wreck yours. Aiden's death has been tough on all of us. However, that is not the end of the world. It's already been months, you have not been outside, and now you scarcely talk to me. You have also stopped playing your guitar. I know how much you love it. Move on, Jace. You are wasting yourself. Please,' she prays in a jittery tone, 'I don't want to lose you, too.'

I merely nod because God knows she is right.

'You leave for rehab next week,' she says. 'That okay?' she inquires with tears on the rims of her peepers.

I don't have the heart to turn her down, so I nod again.

'It's for your own good, Jace. It will not be as awful as you expect,' Pearl tells me as she helps me stuff my clothes into my suitcase.

Tomorrow I depart for rehab and I'm already dreading the thought of it. However, Pearl insists it's the best thing for me. My mind drifts to how life would have been if Aiden were still alive. Perhaps we would have been on another tour or at a press conference. A smile fluctuates on my lips as I recall how everything was before the tragic event.

Minnesota Rehabilitation Centre is written boldly at the entrance of the building. Pearl grips my hand as the driver enters the parking lot. When he finally finds a space, we alight from the car. A lady in a grey dress walks up to us with a pleasant smile on her face. She has pretty, blonde hair, like mine.

'Hello, Miss Tanner. I'm Theresa. Dr Maria asked me to see you in.' Her smile was still intact. 'You can follow me now.' She turns and starts walking while Pearl and I tag along at her back.

We wait for a few minutes at the reception before being called inside. A Black woman, whom I assume to be Dr Maria, is sitting on the sofa in the office. *She looks friendly.* Maybe Pearl was right. Perhaps this place is not as uninviting as I thought. Her face lights up when she notices our presence.

'Hello!' she greets us with a smile as she points her fingers to the sofa, asking us to sit. 'I'm Dr Maria. It's nice to finally meet you, Jace. Pearl has told me so much about you.' I don't say a word. Pearl hits me with her elbow and asks me to stop being rude. She clears her throat. 'All payments are clear, so you only have to sign some papers, then we'll have Jace taken to his apartment,' she states.

'That is good. Can we sign now?' Pearl asks.

'Yes, definitely,' she replies and slides the paperwork to our side of the table.

After Pearl finishes reading the paperwork, she signs where necessary. Dr Maria tells us that visiting is only allowed on Thursdays and Saturdays and assures Pearl that I'll be a new person by the time I leave. I just sit there and roll my eyes as they talk. When they're finished, we head to the apartment. It isn't as bad as I thought it would be. Pearl paid a fortune to ensure I had the best apartment here.

A few hours and a million words of encouragement later, Pearl leaves. I fold my clothes and put them in the mini closet, but just as I begin to enjoy my peace and serenity, I hear a knock and grumble as I walk to the door to unlock it. Dr Maria appears. She walks in and looks around.

'I see you are getting comfortable already,' she smiles softly at me and then sits. 'Different people like you have been here. Some have been through worse than you have, addictions that were worse than yours. I'm happy that I could help them change, help them change their lives, and get the life they truly deserved. I'll be happy if I can achieve that with you, and it will only be possible if you are ready to do that with me. It can only happen if you prepare to let go of your past. Hard? Of course, it will be, but it's very possible.'

Surprisingly, Doc's speech touches me.

'I wouldn't be here if I were not ready for a change, Dr Maria,' I retort.

'You're trying to put on a facade of being all right. How is that going for you, Jace?' she replies calmly. I hate how she can see through all of my actions; she makes me feel naked. 'We will have a private session tomorrow morning at 10am. Have a pleasant night, Jace.'

She lets herself out without even giving me a chance to respond. A loud sigh comes out of my mouth, and I make my way to the bed and lay down. Different thoughts run through my mind. I eventually give up and let sleep pull me in.

A loud noise jerks me awake from my troubled sleep. I shut my eyes harder and turn to the other side of the bed, but the noise persists. The time must be 6am. The routine says 6am is workout time, so I reluctantly get up and head to the toilet to pee and brush my teeth. I throw on one of Aiden's shirts and sweatpants that I had taken from him when he was alive, wanting to feel like he is with me. I drag my feet as I move to join the other people already in the gym.

'First day, eh?' I hear someone say to me. I turn to see a thin man of average height with a neatly trimmed beard.

'Is it that obvious?' I reply.

He chuckles. 'I can always tell. I'm Sam,' he says.

'Jace,' I answer, and we shake hands.

Sam helps me with my workout and tells me to take things easy since it's my first day. When it's 7.30am, the alarm goes off again, signalling the end of our workout session. I thank Sam and head to my room for a much-needed shower.

Oat bread, eggs, and avocado are for breakfast, but I eat little. I have barely eaten since Aiden's death. The drugs are my only companion. I decide to explore parts of the facility before my appointment with Dr Maria, so I take a stroll around the garden. The cool morning breeze hits me as I step back slowly into the main building. A beautiful painting hanging on the wall makes me stop in my tracks. Aiden loved art in all its forms. A soft smile finds its way to my lips as I use my hands to caress the canvas on display.

'You like art?' A voice interrupts. I turn to see Dr Maria. 'I looked for you everywhere. I thought you ran away,' the doc says again.

'No, but my friend Aiden, he always admired art,' I respond.

'Why don't we talk about this, Aiden, in my office?'

We walk to her office in silence. She opens the door, and I let myself in. I sit on the sofa, making myself comfortable.

'So, Jace, is there anything you would like?' she asks.

'No,' I reply.

'Okay then, we will start now. How do you feel today, Jace?'

'Great, just great,' I sigh. 'I don't know how I feel. Mixed emotions. I feel empty. I miss my best friend. I miss making music, and I blame myself for his death,' I exhale.

'You talked about a certain Aiden downstairs. Do you mind telling me about him?'

Picturing Aiden right here with us leads to a lop-sided smile on my gab.

'Aiden was my best friend. He had dark curly hair and a crooked nose that he got from fighting in seventh grade.' I smile slightly at the memory of him fighting. 'He was about four inches taller than I am and claimed to be older because of this, but we're agemates. Our parents died in a car crash around the same time. They were friends too, and we were inseparable since then. We did everything together so much that we even started making music together. I wish we didn't take cocaine that day. The doctor said it made him bleed internally. That is how Aiden died.' Tears roll down my eyes. Dr Maria does not interrupt my crying, and she tells me to let it all out. She clasps my hands, trying to comfort me.

'Why do you constantly blame yourself for his death?' she asks.

'Pearl warned us about drugs! He wanted to quit, but I persuaded him not to. I gave him the sugar that killed him. How am I not to be blamed?' I continue sobbing.

'Jace, you look sullen. I know you think you have lost it all. If we go on this trip of self-actualisation, we need to do it jointly. I'll be with you every step of the way,' she whispers.

Something about her makes me feel secure enough to let all my demons out. We chat about Russ and Cross and whether I'd like to return to university. We also talk about continuing with Soft Division, but I just don't know yet. She informs me of the music room on the second floor. Slowly, I gain a liking for Dr Maria.

After my session with Dr Maria, I head to the dining area to have lunch consisting of broccoli, lettuce, olives, and chicken. When I get back to my apartment, I see my guitar on the couch in my living room.

'How did this land here?' I murmur to myself while picking up the guitar. Aiden gave it to me for my birthday last year. I notice a note taped on the back of the guitar.

He would want you to have this with you. Saw it while I was cleaning your den and dropped it off. Love you. Pearl.

After reading the note Pearl left me. I sit on the couch and strum the guitar. I played some songs Aiden and I created together before we started Soft Division. This helps me to feel at peace with myself. I play an array of different notes before I take a nap.

A quick nap eventually turns into a heavy slumber of four hours. I enjoy the sense of waking up like a different man. I make my way to the facility library, taking the book Dr Maria gave me. *The Road to Self-realisation*, she penned it herself. I hardly read three pages before I start yawning, so I abandon the book and shift to face the library window. *This place is lovely*. My agony has left me empty enough not to notice the little things anymore. Minutes turn to hours, hours turn to days, days turn into weeks, weeks turn to seasons.

It has been six months since I arrived at the Minnesota rehabilitation centre. I have made a few friends; Dr Maria, the receptionist, Theresa, Lily, and Craig; I take the same addiction management classes with those two, and Sam, whom I met on my first day. Craig had worse addictions than the other three of us. Lily was an alcoholic before, but the addiction management classes are helping her. Sam somewhat reminds me of Aiden. He told me a few days ago that he was like an African wild dog and depended on crack to live his life. I connected with them during these few months because I found people like myself. Pearl visited me once a month. The apartment had turned into my sanctuary, and the painting downstairs was still reminiscent of Aiden. Today, I leave the Minnesota rehab centre as a different man, a different being. I feel super optimistic as I organise my suitcases. There is a hammer on the door.

'It's open,' I hoot, and in walks Dr Maria. Trust her to want to talk to me at a time like this.

'Oh, Jace! Pearl is here already,' she announces, and Pearl pops up from behind her and tugs me into a tight hug.

Her strawberry scent hits my nostrils as I let her caress me, just like every time we met before. I try to be as excited as I can to reciprocate her sentiments of affection. It has been six months. She vowed to fetch me when it was time to leave rehab. She kept her promise.

'I can't wait to take you home!' she says gleefully.

'Short hair suits you,' I say to Pearl. The bob cut suits her dainty shoulders, and the crimson streaks at the end compliment her ivory skin. She readjusts the hoodie on her waistline and beams. A compliment from me was as rare as a hen with teeth.

'Glad to know they knocked some sense into you,' she chuckles, flipping her head backwards. I scrunch up my nose. I can't help but grin, too, because I have been waiting for this day.

'Before you leave, Lily, Craig, Theresa, and Sam asked to see you,' she informs me. I smile and excuse myself to go meet them.

'Jace!' Lily exclaims as she sees me, rushing to where I stand. The other three come walking behind her.

'We're going to miss you, Jace. Just make sure you stay in touch when you are out there,' Theresa says, and I salute.

Craig hands me a box. I open it, and inside is a small picture of the four of us. I smile, and before I realise, tears roll down my cheeks.

Pearl and I exit the rehab centre and head towards the parking lot.

'I thought I would have to deal with your annoying girlfriend on the way home,' I pester her as we pace towards the red Range Rover. She seems to be infatuated with red these days. That's Pearl for you. She likes to keep up with the trends.

'Olivia and I split up,' Pearl replies, shrugging it off as we get into the car.

'What happened to being with her is different and blah blah blah?' I mock, shutting the door with a thud. Her hand is on the wheel as she turns, removing her car from the parking lot. Her eyes trained behind.

'She cheated on me,' Pearl simply comes back with.

My eyes go wide, and I decide not to wreck her mood by speaking about Olivia. I know she will open up to me eventually. I howl as I try to soak up everything. It has been six months since I last sat inside a car. I spread myself on the seat, watching Pearl as she drives us home. The drive home is silent. I stare at the unusual buildings as we cruise through. Places I used to know now look very unfamiliar.

'We're home, Jace. What are you pondering over?' Pearl disrupts my thoughts as she parks the car.

I clear my throat and mouth, 'nothing.'

We descend from the Range Rover and walk to the front porch. I continue to stare at everything as Pearl unlocks the door, still in awe of everything. It must be because I haven't been outside of rehab for six months.

'Take your suitcases to your den, Jace. I'll make you something to nibble on. Then we will chat. We have a lot to talk about,' Pearl says breathlessly.

I take a deep sigh and do as she asks. This was the room that I lived in before moving to my apartment. I vividly recall the good old times all four of us had while rehearsing in this den. We killed time making great music and understanding our rhythm. Oh my, how tempus fugit! I make my way to the bathroom for a quick shower, throw on a white shirt and blue jeans, and head downstairs. The aroma of Pearl's food fills my nostrils.

'Mmmm, sis! What is cooking?'

I say as I stroll into the kitchen. I try to sneak and steal a hotdog from the plate on the kitchen counter. My sister is sharp enough to strike me with the spoon in her hand.

'Pearl!' I whine before stomping out of the kitchen like a little boy. 'Just like old times,' I say to myself with a smile.

I turn on the TV in the living area, and a news channel comes on.

'We're live at the Backwoods band concert! The biggest concert this season. Since the collapse of Soft Division last year, I don't think there has been a stronger replacement for them,' the reporter announces.

An immediate sense of numbness overwhelms me. I immediately turn off the TV and lay back on the couch.

'Backwoods,' I scoff and roll my eyes.

Instantly, my mind drifted to happier times about our song that was number one for two successive seasons.

'Here we go, about time how it flew

It's just me left without you

You played me, baby, like you play everybody

Looked so classy, but now you're just somebody,' I hum it.

The memory of us making the song in Aiden's garage ran in front of my eyes. I vaguely remember how we made fun of Cross for falling in love with a girl we all knew was seeing every other guy in college. It was epic watching his reaction when she threw iced coffee on him while he tried to court her in front of the whole college. We felt terrible for him, and that was how this melodramatic song was born. I wonder what he is doing in his life now. If I had the strength left in me, I would run to his place and have a cup of tea, over which we could discuss our good old days. Therapy took the surviving parts of my soul, and I don't know if there is a cure.

'I have fixed us supper. Jace! Come over here,' Pearl calls. I linger a few minutes before I rise. When I get to the dining table, I meet Pearl already seated, waiting for me to park my rear. 'Dig in,' she says to me.

I don't need an invitation; I have been starving since the drive home. Pearl and I converse about various things while we dine. I decide to ask about the Backwoods. She should at least know a bit about them.

'Backwoods? They are the new boys on the block and already have two songs on the Billboard charts. You will love their music. We should attend one of their concerts, don't you think?' answers Pearl.

I suddenly feel envious, imagining "Backwoods" looting the life I once had. I keep branding myself as a disappointment, which is a dangerous feeling, and recall the discussions I had with Dr Maria about my "self-blame issue."

'Hey, do you mind if I visit Aiden tomorrow?' I ask, switching the conversation.

'Why not? Let me know if you need a ride there. I'll be glad to help,' Pearl responds.

I load the dishes into the dishwasher and scurry back to my den.

I wake up early the following day and decide to jog around the neighbourhood. I'm used to working out now as it helps me keep my head clear at the start of a new day. After my jog, I help myself to a mug of cappuccino in the kitchen. Pearl comes down a few minutes later.

'You have been out this morning,' she says, clearly

surprised. I pull out another mug to make her coffee.

'Well, an alternative lifestyle,' I declare, beaming.

'Impressive. The rehab is worth all the fat dollars. Still going to see Aiden?' she asks.

'Yes.'

'Jace, people already know that you are in town. Be careful around those reporters today, okay?' she discloses.

I nod my head in acknowledgement and dart up the stairs to get ready for my day. I'm feeling rather impatient to see my best buddy's grave and talk to him about how I feel. I take a quick shower and throw on my clothes. Since I'll be spending the entire day outside, I pick up a bag to put some snacks in.

It takes time for me to find my way to the cemetery, but I eventually do. By the time I get to the gates, I'm shaking.

'You can do this, Jace,' I mumble to myself, trying to muster up some grit.

I finally walk in and trace my steps to Aiden's grave. A sigh of relief escapes me when I find it. I smile and perch on it. Somehow, that sense of dread is long gone.

'Hey bro. It's me, Jace,' I exhale. 'I hope you are good over there. I can still feel you here right now. It still seems like a bad dream that I can't wake up from, but Pearl claims this is real. Life has been hell without you, Aiden. A few months after losing you, I had to go to rehab because it crushed me. I made a few friends there. My therapist, Dr

Maria, was so nice to me. Even though I was rude at first, she gave me a chance. I made a few friends; Lily, Craig, and Sam. I talked about you so much! Sam reminded me of you. Spending six months at a rehabilitation centre sounded ridiculous at first, but it saved me. I still blame myself for losing you.' My voice breaks because I'm sobbing. 'Anyhow, I'm back home. It all seemed good until I heard about the Backwoods. I feel like a failure all over again. The correspondent on TV said their band is the new "Soft Division." They can never be like us. I miss making music with you. Everywhere looks unfamiliar, presumably because I was away for a while. It feels like the Backwoods stole our lives, and I honestly envy them. I don't know what I'm going to do with my life now, but I'm going to figure it out.'

I smile again as I read the first sentence on his grave.
In loving memory of Aiden Gill.

'I wish I could have time to see you again, Aiden,' I sigh

Tears start falling uncontrollably; I don't dry them. Instead, I let them roll down freely. I lay down on the desolate ground and rest my head on the marble headstone, trying to picture Aiden with me, right here at this moment. The calm wind lingers on my face, and I close my eyes. I feel calm. My eyes open gently, and I realise where I am. I instantly get up and adjust myself before saying bye to Aiden and leaving the burial ground. My visit to Aiden felt comforting. As I continue my walk back home, someone bumps into me.

'Hello!' she calls out, sounding like an inept woman. 'I'm Ella, and you must be Jace! I'm a columnist.'

Before I know it, more of them pop out from distant intersections of the lanes, leaving me feeling shaken.

'Do you want to pursue your music career again?'

'Don't you feel like you are just another artist who got trounced by the sombre hand of the industry?'

'Where are your other bandmates?'

I answer none of their questions, and I charge back home to escape their grills.

'You did not tell me how absurd those reporters can be,' I yell as I barge into the house. The reporters followed me to my front door.

Pearl only lets out a slight snicker. 'Now, now, don't get grouchy, Jace. You should get used to it,' she adds.

I grab a seat next to her on the three-seater couch.

'How did your day go?' she asks me.

'Speaking to Aiden made me feel better than expected,' I answer honestly.

'Okay, baby brother,' she says, engrossed in whatever TV show she is watching.

I head upstairs to shower whilst trying to figure out my next line of action. Do I go on and pursue my dreams? Do I drop everything from my past and pick up a new hobby?

I'm at crossroads now. After freshening up, I sit with Pearl to watch one of her soap operas.

'I have some news, Jace,' she informs me.

'I'm all ears.'

'I have been considering going on a trip with you so you can get comfortable again and maybe rediscover yourself.' Sometimes, it's almost as if Pearl reads my mind.

'A trip to where?' I question.

'We will be exploring the whole of Europe for 15 days,' she claims.

'Europe? 15 days? Isn't that too far-fetched?' I inquire.

'Trust me. You will love it! I promise you will. I think you require some time away from Minnesota, so this is a good opportunity.'

At this stage, I can't help but agree.

'I'll trust you on this one, Pearl,' I say to her with a cramped grin. She stands up and waltzes around.

The following day, Pearl leaves early to meet with her travelling company. I'm alone at home, so I decide to strum my guitar. I scribble some lyrics while I practice. A tap on the door interrupts my session, and I scramble to the door to see who it is.

'Open up, Jace!' As soon as I figure it's Pearl, I immediately unlock the door and let her in. 'We're good to go!' she spits out as soon as she is inside.

'I don't follow you.'

'We're good to go to Europe!' She yells again.

'Settle down, Pearl. When do we take off?' I ask.

'Next week. I have already arranged for the documents. Get ready for the best 15 days of your life,' Pearl exclaims, sounding elated.

'Okay, sis,' I snicker, and I pick up my guitar and head into my den.

'Are all your bags in?' Pearl questions for the millionth time today.

We're leaving for the airport and Pearl is this close to making us miss our flight because she is fidgeting to ensure everything is proper. Knowing she still forgets things.

When we get to the airport, she hurries off to the checkpoint, shows them our tickets, and checks us in. We hand over our baggage and then proceed into the departure lounge. It takes a while to locate our boarding gate, but we ultimately find it. We wait in the queue to board the airplane. Once we board, I let out a sigh of relief, feeling drained from racing around. I struggle to elude the thought of sitting for nine hours while flying to Europe. Pearl keeps on blabbering about how much I'll love Europe once I'm there. The whole nine hours seem too long. When the captain informs us that we will touch down in a few minutes, I internally jump. We all descend from the craft one by one at our first destination, Paris,

France. The capital of passion.

'Will I ever find love?' I ask myself.

Once out of the airport, we hail a taxi that comes to a halt in front of us.

'Grand Hotel Dechampagne,' she informs the chauffeur.

He snorts, 'Grand Hotel Dechampaigne,' correcting us and then drives us to our hotel.

The driver turns on the music in his car, so the drive isn't boring. I bob my head to the piece of music until we arrive at the hotel, where we descend from the taxi and pay the chauffeur. The exterior is magnificent. I suddenly wonder how splendid the interior will be. We receive our keys from reception, give our bags to the porter, and follow him as he leads us to our rooms. Pearl's room is directly opposite mine. Pearl lets out a slight giggle, obviously ecstatic that she is now travelling around Europe. I step into my room and stare in awe around the place. Feeling jet-lagged, I decide to take a quick shower and nap.

'Let's go! The other tourists are waiting,' Pearl screeches in my ear while I'm asleep.

I instantly get on my feet and follow her outside to wait for our coach.

'There!' Pearl yells and skips to the bus.

I growl in exasperation and follow her. When we get on to the bus, there's mumbles of 'good morning,' from the other tourists. It isn't long until the coach comes to a halt right at the entrance of the Louvre Museum. I have read various articles about this place being the finest museum, and I'm about to witness it for myself. We all stand outside, waiting for our tour guide to turn up.

'Hello, tourists!' A graceful female voice speaks from afar.

A lady in a classic blue dress walks over to our group. She has blue eyes, complimenting her attire, tumbling black hair, and a lithe waistline. The shape of her face is oval, her lips are full, and the most delicate I have ever seen. A necklace settles just below her collarbone and dimples appear on each side of her cheeks as she speaks.

Damn! I think to myself. *This is such a charming woman.*

'I'm sorry for being late. The actual tour guide had to cancel, so I'm his replacement. Don't fret. You will love me!' she humours. 'I'm Yasmine Belmont. Your tour guide for today, and we're here at the Louvre Museum! I would love to know your names, but I suppose that can wait. Let us head into the museum,' she speaks confidently, which is alluring. 'On my first visit to the Louvre, I went inside without a guide, but I learnt my lesson. So, my second time, I went inside with a guide, and it was well worth it.' She talks about the Louvre and shows us around. 'The Louvre is so vast that it will take you nine months to walk through, and twenty-four hours a day to study it all. Better to go on a guided tour,' she advises us. 'You might be wondering why the Louvre is so popular? Well, The Louvre is more than just an art museum. It was originally a medieval fortress. It was also the royal palace of France until the monarchy shifted to Versailles. As the French revolution approached its last stages, the National Assembly turned it into a museum to showcase over five hundred masterpieces of art. Despite having to shut down several times at various stages in history, the Louvre constantly gathered an assortment of approximately 568,000 art pieces dating from ancient times to the 1850s, 38,000 of which are on display. It's known universally for Leonardo da Vinci's Mona Lisa and I. M. Pei's glass pyramid. The glass pyramid has served as the museum's main entrance since 1988 and is an instantly recognisable landmark in Paris,' she explains carefully.

I honestly can't help but adore her intellect. I tip my head to see if Pearl is looking at me, but she is not. She is busy taking pictures. Yasmine takes us to the front of a sculpture. Even if I don't know a thing about art, I try to tune in because I crave to load my ears with her charming silken voice. God! I'm positive I sound like a stalker.

'The Louvre's grand exhibition space sprawls across nearly 18 acres and has 403 rooms spread over three wings on multiple levels. A myriad of staircases connects these wings. No one can finish exploring it in a single day. Every few hours spent going around can be a hectic workout, even for the fittest lot,' Yasmine repeats. 'Who wishes to see the Mona Lisa painting?' she exclaims. The others gasp and yell a big 'yes,' in unison. 'It would be challenging and virtually impossible for someone to do a complete tour of the Louvre in a limited amount of time. Even the briefest visits involve a great deal of attention and effort, considering that the individual visiting would have to walk for most of the tour and that they would have to pay close attention to the artwork that they are interested in,' she adds. We come to a stop right in front of the Mona Lisa painting. 'Leonardo da Vinci's Mona Lisa is considered one of the most treasured paintings by art enthusiasts from around the world, and today it hangs in the Louvre Museum right here in Paris. This piece of art is recognised as one of the most outstanding works ever created by any artist; it serves as a contemporary object of pilgrimage for people worldwide. It's universally believed that the masterpiece was created between 1503 and 1519 by da Vinci when he resided in Florence. Ever since the creation of the Mona Lisa in the 16th century, it has become a well-respected piece of art, influencing many artists from the past, present, and wishfully the future. Mystery has always shrouded The Mona Lisa. Various aspects of the painting beg for deeper examination and are a source of enchantment for enthusiasts,' she educates us on the painting. 'The Mona Lisa has to be one of my favourite paintings of all time. Della Gioconda, The Mona Lisa, is undoubtedly the most famous piece of art in the world. Shortly after the paintings' creation, its previously unattainable levels of skill, technique, and realism attracted widespread adoration. To this day, the public's infatuation with the artwork is nothing short of incredible,' she continues as she turns away to let the tourists take pictures.

She walks in front of us and continues to speak about various paintings like the wedding of Cana, Titian's pastoral concert, and lots more.

'The greatest Venetian painters once shared a love for vibrant and spectacular colours. Veronese's monumental Wedding Feast at Cana is displayed opposite the Mona Lisa, and other artistic masterpieces surround it. Masterpieces such as Titian's Pastoral Concert and Man with a Glove, Tintoretto's vigorous sketch especially made for The Coronation of the Virgin or Paradise (part of a vast artistic plan for the Sala del Maggiore Consiglio in the Doge's Palace in Venice), fantastic portraits such as Veronese's Portrait of a Venetian Woman, known as La Bella Nani, and many more brilliant pieces of artistic delight. A burst of bright light and dazzling colours reflects the extraordinary skills of Venetian Renaissance artists,' she elaborates.

I can't help but admire her intelligence. She seems to be around my age, too.

'We should take a quick break. Let's gather back here in thirty minutes,' Yasmine says.

Pearl is the first to hurry off. One can tell she is famished. While Yasmine stands, I move to her to make small talk.

'Hi, Yasmine!' I beam and walk up to her.

She sends a smile my way, showing her even white teeth, before responding to my greeting.

'Hello, you must be one of the tourists,' she says, and I nod.

'You kind of look familiar,' she adds. She probably knows me from Soft Division. 'I'll figure out where I know you from. Don't worry. I hope you are enjoying the tour?'

'Yes, I'm Jace, Jace Tanner,' I smile as I say my name, hoping she does not remember.

'Okay, Jace,' she smiles, and her lovely dimples appear on her face once again.

I compliment her and let her know I love how she elaborates on every painting we have stumbled upon during the tour. Within twenty minutes, I make a good impression of myself with Yasmine Belmont. Everybody arrives from their break but gives them time to rest before she proceeds again.

'Did you know that The Wedding Feast at Cana is the largest painting in the Louvre? It's over six meters high and ten metres wide. It depicts an exuberant banquet with a gathering of over one hundred and thirty distinct characters in a blaze of lights and colours. Veronese painted the scene for the monastery's refectory on the island of San Giorgio Maggiore in Venice. In 1798, Dictator Napoleon's troops confiscated the painting and shipped it to Paris. After the downfall of his Empire in 1815, most of the confiscated pieces of art were returned to Italy; fearing that "The Wedding Feast" may not survive its journey back home, France kept it in exchange for a painting by Charles Le Brun. Despite all this, Veronese's huge masterpiece had to be moved twice in later years, when Paris was at war in 1870 and 1939.' We stop at the painting, The raft of Medusa. 'The raft of Medusa was painted by Théodore Géricault depicting the survivors of a shipwreck adrift and starving on a raft. Géricault astonished viewers by painting, in harrowing detail, not an antique and noble subject but a recent gruesome incident.'

I wonder how she knows such intricate details about paintings and history, so much so that it forces me to ask her about it. I raise my hand.

'Yes, Jace,' she says with a smile.

She remembers my name, I think happily.

'How come you know so much about these paintings, and yet you are not even a real tour guide?' I question.

Pearl sends me a look that reads, 'you will embarrass yourself,' but I ignore her.

'Oh! I'm a historical conservationist by profession.

Besides, my mum owns this tour guide company, so it's only natural to be in the family business,' she states. 'We're going to be seeing the last sculpture of the day, and that is The Venus de Milo,' she exclaims happily. 'Venus de Milo is an ancient statue commonly thought to represent Aphrodite,' she says and then pauses as we stand in front of the sculpture. 'It was carved in marble by Alexandros, a sculptor of Antioch on the Maeander River around 150 BC and was discovered in pieces on the Aegean island of Melos on April eighth, 1820. It was presented to Louis XVIII (who then donated it to the Louvre in 1821), taking immense skill just to reconstruct it and erect it. Among the pieces found, the statue's arms are still missing. An inscription not displayed with the statue states that Alexandros, son of Menides, a citizen of Antioch of Maeander, sculpted the statue. The origins of this sculpture point towards the island of Melos, leading some scholars to think she may be Amphitrite, the Greek goddess of the sea,' she continues.

Everybody makes side-talks around.

'Ladies and Gentlemen, we have come to the end of this wonderful excursion today! I enjoyed talking about art with you. Hopefully, I get to be your tour guide some other time,' she remarks and then does a little mock curtsy, and everybody claps.

I'll not lie. I enjoyed the excursion. Perhaps I only enjoyed staring at Yasmine's face, but at least I enjoyed it. We all head back to the museum entrance and wait for the bus to arrive to go back to our various hotels. While waiting, I spot Yasmine waiting too. Could she be waiting for a bus? Why wait for a bus when she can board ours? I approach her.

'Hello, Yasmine,' I smile as I call her. 'I would like to thank you for the beautiful tour you just gave us.'

She lets out a soft giggle that makes my tummy roll.

'You are welcome. I'm just doing my job,' she says.

'Are you waiting for someone?' I ask.

'Yes. I'm waiting for my mum to pick me up. She should be here in a few minutes,' she answers.

'Oh, okay. I would love to see you again, Yasmine,' I express.

'Well, what can I say? If fate concurs to that, who am I to say no?'

'Jace, the bus is here!' Pearl calls out, and I wave at Yasmine, who waves back.

'I saw how you were staring at the pretty tour guide,' Pearl starts as we get on to the bus. 'You like her?' She giggles and continues to torment me throughout the ride.

Maybe I'm into Yasmine. Perhaps it's love at first sight, but I know a force pulls me to her, making me want to know her and do things with her. The bus stops outside the entrance to the hotel, and we alight. Pearl continues to joke about the fact that I stared at Yasmine throughout the excursion.

'I can order room service, or we can go out to get some food and see what they have around here.' I'm too tired from the excursion, and I want to escape further teasing from Pearl.

'Room service,' I answer.

'On it,' Pearl replies, and enters her room. Finally! Some peace of mind.

I take a cold shower and enter my room to rest when there is a knock on the door.

'Open the damn door, Jace,' Pearl yells.

In a panic, I quickly open the door, thinking it's an emergency, just to find Pearl standing there with a tray in her hand. It doesn't take long for me to grab it and start munching on the food.

'You scared me,' I say to her, referring to the way she yelled earlier. She only smiles.

Pearl can be a handful, even childlike. She sticks her tongue out and runs off to the bed. I shake my head and plop on to the couch. Pearl shows me the pictures she took of me, and in all of those pictures, I had my eyes only on Yasmine. It's almost like she put a spell on me.

'If it's meant to be, it will be baby brother. Don't worry,' Pearl assures me.

Pearl falls asleep on my bed after rambling about different things. The only thing I can now think about is

Yasmine and her pretty blue eyes. I don't understand why I'm attracted to her, but I know I am, and I don't plan on patiently waiting until fate brings us together again.

Chapter Two
Yasmine Belmont

I tug on my blue dress as the gentle wind raises it. I'm supposed to be the tour guide for a group of people at the Louvre museum, and now I can't even locate them. While grumbling in frustration, I twist and see a gathering of disoriented individuals. 'There they are!' I mouth and walk to where they all stand.

'Hello, tourists!' I call out as I stand right at their front, seeking to catch their attention. 'I'm Yasmine Belmont, your tour guide for today, and we're here at the Louvre Museum! I would love to know your names, but I suppose that can wait. Let us head into the museum,' I say, confidently leading the way into the museum.

We make our way through the main entrance of the museum. The tour automatically begins the minute we step into the Louvre. I tell them about how I was disorientated on my first visit to the Louvre. My second time, the tour guide took my tour group and me everywhere. Touring the Louvre is often simpler with a guide. I disclose thoroughly to the group of tourists about the history of the Louvre museum. I lecture them on the paintings and sculptures; essentially all the artwork in the Louvre museum. After talking about the museum's largest painting, "The Wedding Feast of Cana," I give them a thirty-minute break. A tall guy steps up to me and introduces himself as Jace Tanner. He has neatly trimmed thick blonde hair, a chiselled jaw, and striking brown eyes that can mesmerise anyone staring at them. He smiles at me. We make small talk, and the exchange becomes slightly awkward. At least he tries to make me chuckle a bit. Soon, other tourists return from their break. He leaves to join his group. As we proceed to the next canvas, Jace raises his hand and asks a question.

'How come you know so much about all these depictions? Since you are not even a real tour guide?' he investigates.

I get questions like these from tourists all the time, but I invariably give the same answer.

'Oh! I'm a historical conservationist by profession. Besides, my mum owns this tour guide company, so it's only natural to be in the family business,' I reply with a smile. I have filled in for absent tour guides on various occasions. Being a historical conservationist also prepared me for the job.

I move to the last stop of this excursion and do a little mock curtsy when I round up the tour, to which everybody cheers. Immediately, some tourists move outside to wait for their bus. Others come up to me and tell me how much they enjoyed the tour and how gracious I was in pointing out all the rare details to them.

I have to stick around for a few minutes before my mum comes to pick me up, so I stand in the parking lot, finding shade under the sweltering sun before a voice startles me. I turn again; it's Jace. Yes Jace, from the tour.

'Hello, Yasmine,' his deep voice sounds so sexy. It makes my insides flutter. He sends a smile my way before speaking again. 'I would like to thank you for the wonderful tour you just gave us.' I let out a biting laugh because I feel charmed.

'You are welcome. I'm just doing my job,' I say to him.

'Are you expecting someone?' he questions. I tell him my mum will be here in a few minutes to pick me up.

'Oh, okay. I would love to see you again, Yasmine,' he says with a curious expression in his eyes.

'Well, what can I say? If fate concurs to that, who am I to say no?' I respond.

Hell! I don't even understand why I said that. I should have sought an exchange of contacts.

'Jace, the bus is here!' a lady yells from afar. He waves, and I wave back before he dashes to the parked bus.

Who was that lady? His girlfriend? A friend? His sister? I question myself, somehow worrying that I'm even asking myself this. Why do I care? He is only a stranger who I met today. Who knew if I would have the chance to see him again? While I'm speculating, my mobile phone rings. I glance at the caller ID. It's Charlotte!

'Hi, girl! How is it going?' I say with excitement.

'Yasmine, I miss you so much. I'm going crazy without you.' I roll my eyes at her gripes, grateful she can't see me. She is a drama queen.

'Slow down, Charlotte. I'm positive it's not that awful,' I try to soothe her.

'Is a master's degree more important than me?' she whimpers; I giggle at the obvious joke as she laughs on the other end of the phone.

'Work feels empty without you. Everyone misses you,' she says.

'I miss you more, Charlotte. Let's hang out together this weekend and guess what?' I tease her.

'What?' she squeals with delight.

'I...'

'...I have to go now. Make sure you call me tonight. I want to hear everything,' she cuts in.

We say our quick goodbyes. Charlotte and I used to work together, and we became tight at work. She is a lovely young woman. My mum loves her too. She is older than I am, but we're good buddies. I resigned from my place of work because I intend to get a master's degree, and I have to prepare for my exams to get in. Any job I choose right now will have to be part-time, and my previous workplace had no such arrangements available. I enjoyed my job at the art gallery because I admire art and love speaking to people about it. I have met different people with rare insights about art almost every day. It goaded me to work every day because I knew that at least one guy would look at a painting or an antique differently. I also like to examine new artefacts and relics brought in and carry out research about them. It's an intriguing task.

A few minutes after Charlotte hangs up, my mum's car comes to a halt right in front of me. My mum looks young for her age. At forty-two, she still retains a banging body that makes men drool. I inherited my long, tumbling hair from her. Her smile could quell the Parisian Conciergerie clock.

'Took you long enough.' I roll my eyes as I hop into her car, and we speed off.

'How was the tour, ma Cherie?' She inquires.

'Beautiful, satisfied tourists!'

'Yay! Yasmine to the rescue!' she laughs, making me smile for the first time since I spoke to Charlotte.

Finally, we reach our home. I descend from the car and barge into the house because Mum almost always leaves the door unlocked. The nerve of that woman to think no one could rob us. We were not wealthy, but we could afford the good things in life.

When I was younger, we went through a lot, from having issues with my dad to moving to Paris with my mum and starting anew. When I was a kid, my parents were together. My old man is an American, and my mum is from France. It was a beautiful home, just the three of us. I was a daddy's girl; he loved and adored me. He would get me presents, even when it was not my birthday or any special occasion. My parents struggled to have other children, but the miscarriages kept on happening. Nonetheless, we were one peaceful family. My parents lived in marital bliss until my dad lost his job. He started staying out late at first, boozing and coming home drunk. Every time Mum tried to warn him, he howled at her to let him be. Gradually, he started spending weekends away from home; weekends turned into weeks. He continued drinking alcohol. My dad stopped caring about us. Then the abuse started, verbally at first. He would call my mum names and criticise her for his life's woes. He would come back to apologise after sobering up, sobbing, and begging my mum to help him. It turned into a cycle: drink, abuse, apologise and repeat. One afternoon, he arrived home smelling like a drum of moonshine. Mum was struggling to talk to him. He shoved her off and suddenly whacked her. From then, my mum turned into a punching bag for him. He mistreated my mum constantly, and she endured it because she admired him. She believed the man she cherished was somewhere in this beast. Until one unfortunate night, he again got home very drunk and started throwing his usual tantrums. He pulled his belt out and whipped her with it. What could I do? I was only a child. I cowered in a corner and bit my lip until I drew blood, praying for this frightful moment to be over. He picked up the knife that was by the side table, as if the belt was not enough. At first, I assumed he would merely scare her with it, but he held it closer to her neck. I saw my mum freeze with disbelief in her eyes. It petrified me, and I knew I had to do something. I did not know what. Then it dawned on me. The police! Mum had taught me the number to call in case of emergencies. I galloped to the phone and dialled 911, howling for help. I won't lie; that was the bravest decision of my life. I hate to imagine what might have transpired if I had not made that choice. The police showed up at our house a few minutes later and then an ambulance. Although he did not slash her throat, he severely injured my mum with all the beatings he had doled out to her. They found out at the hospital that my mum was pregnant, which she didn't know herself, but she lost her baby because of the abuse she suffered at my dad's hands. His arrest led to the court charging him with domestic battery. My mum still pleaded to drop all charges against him with everything he did. Since she was the victim, the court complied, but there was a restraining order from the court. My mum moved to Paris after they separated, and I left with her because I could never look at my father in the same light again. This incident gave me nightmares for many years, traumatising me.

We lived with my grandmother for a few years in Paris before she passed on. Maman, as we called her, was sweet and supportive. Starting all over was tough for my mum, coupled with the fact that she had me to deal with too.

She circled advertisements for jobs in newspapers every day and went for numerous interviews. When she finally found a job, she got fired after two weeks. She constantly looked at the sunnier side of everything. I like to think I got most of my traits from her. When Maman died, I was just twelve, so my mum and I had to move to our apartment. After some years, my father tried to reach us, but my mum decided we wanted nothing to do with him. Mum decided she wanted to establish her own business, as she loved to travel, and she loved art. My mum is a surprisingly optimistic woman, and that optimism always held her down anytime she was in distress. I constantly see myself in her. I believe I inherited all her virtues, plus her striking looks. Eventually, she set up a tourist services company from scratch, and now, we own one of the most famous tourist services in Europe. I love to help her every once in a while, when I can. For instance, today I replaced an absent tour guide. I have done that often since I quit my position at the art gallery downtown.

'A penny for your thoughts?' my mum's voice jolts me back to reality. 'What are you pondering over?' she asks, beaming so brightly that the corners of her eyes crinkle.

'Nothing,' I retort.

I shuffle to the fridge in the kitchen and take out my leftover sandwich from this morning. I gnaw on it. It still tastes fresh. It's not like I care. All I crave is to have something in my mouth.

'You did not tell me about the tour,' my mum says, settling on the couch in the living area.

'Nothing unusual. The Louvre is still the Louvre, and I spoke about art to about twenty tourists,' I answer quickly, my mouth still full of sandwich.

Yes, I'm hiding some information, like the guy that urged me to see him again. If I mentioned it to her, I wouldn't hear the end of it. I also know she would blame me for not exchanging contacts. My mum knows how I am about trusting people, especially men. She assumes it has something to do with my father. I can't deny that fact. We have spoken about it, and I'm getting better at trusting people. Aside from that, I have had my share of experiences with men. The first guy I dated was after high school. It was all petals and roses. I even dreamt of marrying him, but subsequently, I found out about a wager set by him to date me, and that was the end of whatever relationship we had. The entire incident forced me to retract into my shell. I chose to be on my own after that awful incident. After considerable persuasion from my mum and the accusation that I was exhausting my youth, I gave dating another shot. Then I found Andrew. He was much older, and he smashed my barriers and drove me to see everything differently. After being with Andrew for roughly a year, I found out Andrew had a wife and a kid that he successfully withheld from me.

It shocked me when I found out, because Andrew did not seem like someone who would cheat. The news shattered me, and I stopped seeing Andrew. Since then, I haven't even attempted to get into another relationship. I have already come to the conclusion that men will continue to break my heart. My mum helped me through it all. I love her so much. After that, I frantically turned down every other guy, and convinced myself that this berserk behaviour was to preserve my inner peace. However, something about Jace Tanner makes me want to drop my shield. The image of Jace warms my core. His blonde hair, his childlike grin, those deep brown eyes, and his rich voice have paved a path into my fantasies. I smile a little, but enough for my dear mother to notice that something is on my mind.

'What are you thinking about?' she quickly asks, wanting to know what caused her daughter to smile that way.

'Nothing, Mum. Just a thought.' I shrug it off.

'Well, a macaron for your thoughts?' My mum sure knows how to obtain answers.

'I met a guy at the museum today. He was one of the sightseers, and he held his stare on me. You know, like a stalker, but this time the good kind of stalker because he was adorable. He stepped up to me after the tour,' I explain.

'Really? What did he say?' Mum asks, already

engrossed in my narrative.

'He said he would like to see me again, and I told him we would have fate decide that. I don't even know what type of response that was, but I know I felt connected to him. Maybe I'll get to see him again,' I sigh after my last word.

My mum only let out a cough, and I know that cough means I did something I could have done differently.

'Don't worry, baby. You will get to see him again. You should have just agreed to exchange contacts. That would have been smoother,' she says, and I could not agree more.

As it's getting late and I've had a long day, I decide to go upstairs for a shower and get into bed.

'Goodnight, Mum,' I say as I peck her goodnight and climb the stairs.

The alarm rings loud in my ear, forcing me to wake up almost instantly, grumblingly reminding myself how I hate mornings. I'm not a morning person at all. I amble down the stairs, and I find my mum standing in front of the kitchen window, overseeing the gardener while he does his job. She is all dressed up in a black suit. Unlike myself, my mum is a morning person. I constantly wonder how she wakes up, takes her bath, and still does her makeup before 8am. She acts like a teen, and here I am at twenty, and I function like an elderly lady. I have my suspicions about that woman.

'Good morning, Mum! What is there for breakfast?' I ask with a grin on my face.

'Must be a perfect morning. You look delighted,' Mum comments as she pulls out her morning paper and begins to read. 'I made waffles for you. They are on the counter,' Mum says, and I quickly rush to the counter to grab my food. If you have not figured it out yet, yes, I love food!

My mum leaves after a few minutes, and I'm left alone at home. I plan to submit my resume to a few places today because staying at home is not what I prefer. I love meeting people and staring at artworks, and I can't do that while sitting at home all day. After bathing and finishing my usual morning drills, I pick out a yellow blouse and black pants, throw them on, style my hair, and get ready to leave. I take another glance at myself in the mirror before stepping out of the house. I decide a cab will be better. It's not like I have another choice, since I don't have a ride of my own. Some of us are just not built to drive. I hail a taxi and get in.

'Musée d'Orsay,' I say, and the driver nods. 'Could you turn the volume up a bit?' I say, and he pumps up the sound. I bob my head to the rhythm of the song playing. Music is another thing I love and I essentially can't go on without it.

The car finally rolls to a stop. I pay the chauffeur

and shift to step into the museum. The Musée d'Orsay is a renowned museum in Paris. It holds many exquisite paintings. At one point, I used to come here to cool off because of how much I love looking at paintings. I run in and head straight to the curator's office. He is a friend of my mum. He invariably makes sure to let me know how welcome I am to work at the Musée d'Orsay, anytime I wish. Mr Martin is such a nice man. I knock on his office door and wait for him to tell me to come in.

'Good morning, Monsieur Martin,' I salute and sit on the armchair in his office.

'Oh hello, Yasmine. To what do I owe this visit?' he queries. He's a forthright man. I appreciate that.

'I'm here to submit my resume. I anticipate there is a part-time job offer like you mentioned, as I can't commit fully,' I confess to the curator. He chuckles, then rises.

'Of course, Yasmine. There is always a job available for you,' he pauses and licks his lips. 'If you crave it bad enough.'

I shoot him a sceptical stare, but he does not get the message as he advances, this time coming closer to me. I shrink in my seat. My patience is already growing thin. He ignores me and continues to come closer, a lustful look in his scans. I bounce up from my chair before he gets to me.

'Yasmine, I...' he says in his slight French cadence.

'I'll slap you if you take another step towards me,' I say

with all the revulsion I can muster. 'You nauseating little hog,' I say, and storm out of his place.

The shock on his face is everything I hope to accomplish. Men never fail to perplex me. Was he going to talk me into having sex with him for a job? I bite my upper lip, something I always do in rage or distress. I quickly telephone my mum, describing everything to her. My mum panics, but I urge her not to bother. I decide to hang for a while to cool off my boiling rage. There's a fountain close by and I turn towards it. Someone taps me from behind. I spin, and I see the most extreme set of brown eyes I have ever encountered. Jace. Maybe he is on another tour. My heart immediately skips a beat when I look at him. Come on, Yasmine, you just had an encounter with a pervert, and now you are about to fall for one again! No can do. I change my whole demeanour.

'What do you want? Are you stalking me now? Everywhere I go, you are there. Leave me the fuck alone, or I'll call the cops,' I snap at him and stomp off.

I go far and hail a taxi, asking him to drive me home. I weep while he drives; I don't understand why I'm breaking down. It is like a storm of stirring sentiments. I'm crying because Mr Martin pissed me off; I'm weeping because men don't deserve any trust, and Jace did not deserve all I said to him. He sought me out, and I snapped at him; I feel awful now. The driver passes me a tissue, and I mouth a thank you to him. *Such a lovely older man,* I think to myself. I arrive home and pay the driver, adding a tip for his remarkable act. I step into the house, rush to my room, take off my clothes, and lay down in bed naked; I desire some quietude. At this stage, I feel like giving up on finding a job. I reminisce about my old job. Mum arrives late; she rushes to visit me upstairs.

'Hey, baby,' she smiles.

'How do you feel now?' she questions, and I let her know I'm fine, even if it is a pretence. She leaves the room, and I sob quietly again. My mum knows not to disturb me at times like these because she knows I always thug it out. Afterwards, I take a shower and head downstairs.

'I'm going to report Martin,' she says.

I tell her not to worry, as reliving the event all over again will not help me. Then I explain to Mum about my chance encounter with Jace, and she tries to comfort me, convincing me I'll meet him again. I could not help but hope so, too. It isn't until I wake up the following day that I realise I fell asleep on the couch in the living room. You know the moment you feel like you are falling from a cliff while you are sleeping and, in reality, you are only falling from the bed. That is how I currently feel. I lazily go up to my room, brush my teeth and wash my face. I linger in my room, on my bed, for a long time before I hear my mum knocking at the door, asking me to come downstairs.

I park myself at the kitchen counter, waiting to find out what my mother has to say.

'I have been thinking, why seek jobs elsewhere when you are the daughter of the CEO of a tourist service firm? What do you think? You can work for me at your convenience while you study for your examinations.'

Joy fills my heart. 'Yes! Yes, Mum! Oh, thank you!' I shout, wearing the biggest grin ever.

'We have to work out a flexible schedule that will help you study and prepare for your exams. Do well to get ready now and let us head to work. I'll introduce you to everyone today,' my mum says with a grin on her face.

I quickly rush upstairs, grab a fresh grey blouse and a straight skirt that emphasises my curves, take a bath, slip on my clothes with much zest, put on red lipstick that I have had since forever, and then run downstairs to show Mum my outfit.

'What do you think?' I ask, twirling.

She smiles and throws me a thumbs up. I make myself a cup of creamy coffee and slurp it all up hastily.

'Shall we?' I gesture to my mum.

'Yes, we shall,' she says, and we step outside.

Mum refuses to lock the door, but I do it anyway. I fear that we will be robbed one of these days because of how casual she has become.

The drive to work is brief. It's hardly a few minutes away

from where we live, and one can even choose to walk. We proceed into the entrance; I have been to this place more times than I can count. But now, it feels just like my first time. The only difference is that I'll be working here now. My mum introduces me to everybody and informs them I'll work with them from now on, albeit part-time. We settle in my mum's office, my working zone for now, and all I do is grin. I plant myself on the armchair in her office.

'So, what do I do now?' I ask.

'A couple of tourists are travelling to the Eiffel Tower. You should take off now. Don't keep them hanging. You can have the car.' She slides the car keys my way.

Two weeks and lots of tour guiding later, I have concluded that I love being a tour guide. I yearn to see historic places and pick up new things. The best part about being a tour guide is seeing unfamiliar sights for free!

Today is Saturday. It's customarily supposed to be our free day, but Mum says she has business to take care of, and I have to do grocery shopping for Thanksgiving dinner. Thanksgiving! They don't celebrate Thanksgiving much in Europe, but Mum and I make sure to do it every year because we were used to celebrating it back in America. Moreover, we have so much to be grateful for in our lives. Usually, we arrange a feast for the employees at our company where we dine and make merry, but Mum decided that she would prefer it to be just me and her this year. All she probably wanted was some alone time with me. I make my way out of the house to a grocery store to shop for some ingredients so I won't have to shop for them at rush hour. I reach the store, stroll to the aisle towards the cooking ingredients, and pick out everything we need. Then I turn to the meat section and toss some turkey into my cart. As I leave the meat section, I see a familiar figure. The square shoulders, the stature, the swag in his gait, and the blonde hair. It's Tanner! I do a vault inside of me.

'A chance to redeem myself,' I murmur under my breath.

I decide to step up to him and invite him for dinner. I muster up the courage and go forward to talk to him, tapping on his shoulder like he did the last time he approached me. I didn't believe I would get to see him again.

'Oh my God!' He exclaims immediately.

His face lights up when he recognises me. Is he that thrilled to see me? He hauls me into a hug. I did not foresee that, not after how I reacted the other day. We both start speaking at the same time.

'I'm so sorry,' I say.

'I tried…' he says.

We laugh.

'You first,' he says, beaming with his white teeth on full display.

I nod. 'I'm so sorry for how I behaved that day. You did not deserve the reaction you got from me. I had a…'

'Bad day?' he cuts in; his eyes are full of kindness.

'Yes. A grim experience. One I would willingly forget,' I reply.

We start walking.

'Let me get that for you.' He points at the cart I'm pushing.

'Thanks, Jace,' I say, thinking of a plan to invite him for dinner.

'Well, I have been looking for you, even though I didn't know where to seek you out,' he says. I cock my head to one side and look at him. Is he joking? He does not look like he is.

'Would the reason for your quest be to chastise me for being rude yesterday, Mr Tanner?' I ask in a whimsical, theatrical manner.

He reacts with a loud laugh; I can't help but laugh.

'Why don't I take you to dinner, and you will find out, Miss Belmont?' he says.

A splendid opportunity. I do a short, triumphant dance in my mind.

'Hmm, would you like to accompany my mum and me for Thanksgiving dinner?'

An astonishing look crosses his face.

'I thought Thanksgiving is an American thing,' he replies.

'Well, it is. I'm half American. We lived in America before we moved to France. It's a custom we're used to.'

'We have something in common then. I'm from America.'

'I can tell from your pronunciation,' I reply.

We're in the parking lot of the grocery store now.

'You have not acknowledged my invitation,' I tell him.

'Your grace must have carried me away. Forgive me, my lady,' He does a mock surrender. This time, I'm the one to chuckle out heavily.

'Is it okay if I show up with my sister?' he asks.

That must be the female with him the other day.

'Yes, it's absolutely fine,' I reply. Jace helps me haul my shopping into the car.

'I apologise. I'm not much of a skilful driver.'

'I have little choice, don't I?' he says. I grin, and we continue to talk while I steer us out of the grocery store.

'So, are you here on holiday?' I ask.

'Yes, we are. My sister and I. She recommended it to me, and I figured I could use a holiday,' he answers.

'Great. How many days are you here for?'

'Just a few.'

'Oh, I know some fascinating places. I can be your guide,' I say with a playful smile.

'Oh, wow. I didn't know you offer tour guide services. Hope your costs are affordable?' he answers sarcastically, and we both laugh at the banter.

'We're here,' I announce as we arrive at the apartment I live in with my mum. I think Mum is already home, but I'm unsure.

'Can I help you take this inside?' he asks, pointing at the shopping paper bags.

'No, it's fine. You have helped so much already. Thank you. You know where to come tomorrow. Dinner is by six. Don't be late!' I say.

'Miss Belmont, now that destiny has drawn us closer again, I assume you don't mind exchanging contacts with me.'

I laugh and tell him we could exchange contacts now. He informs me they are staying at the hotel Dechampaigne and gives me his room's phone number before disappearing. I love how that went. I enter the house and drop the groceries on the kitchen counter.

'Oh, you are back.' My mum startles me out of nowhere.

'Don't sneak up on me like that, Mum,' I shriek. 'You startled me.'

'Sorry, sorry,' she says, lifting her palms and laughing. That woman gets on my nerves sometimes.

'Guess who I bumped into?' I ask rhetorically, even though I know she would never guess correctly.

'I don't know. Who?' Mum says, and I roll my eyes before speaking again.

'I met Jace!' I exclaim.

'Wow! Where? How?' my mum asks, interested.

'Okay, so, there I was shopping for what we need for dinner tomorrow, and I saw the back view of this blonde. From his features, I could tell he was the one, so I tested if my instincts were right. My instincts had not failed me because he looked glad to see me again. I invited him over for Thanksgiving tomorrow. He and his sister. I hope you don't mind?' I conclude, cocking my head to one side as I make my finishing statement.

'Oh my God! Yasmine, this is wonderful! We will have company. Make sure to inform Charlotte,' she says, smiling ever so broadly.

'I thought you would be furious because you wanted just the two of us to have dinner,' I reply, struggling to mask the bliss I feel after getting her approval. I knew she wouldn't object. She is a social butterfly. I hug my mum so tightly. I love this woman so much. 'Thank you, Mum; you have always been so supportive of me. I love you so much.'

'I love you too, honey. Time to put the groceries away,'

she says.

I roll my eyes and then arrange the groceries in their places.

'Brrrrrrr,' I hear my mobile phone ringing. I fly to pick it up.

'It's him,' I mouth to my mum; she laughs and sways her head at my passion.

'Hey,' the voice on the phone sounds raspy. I could tell who it was.

'Hi,' I answer, a slight smile is playing on my lips, and I feel thankful he is not here to witness this ticklish moment.

'Am I speaking with Yasmine Belmont?' he asks

'Wrong number,' I answer in a proper French accent.

'Nice try,' he says between snickers.

'There's no way you can tell it's me. I perfected my French accent a long time ago.'

'Well, guess what? I can. I feel like I have known you all my life.' Silence. I don't mean to make things unpleasant. I just don't know what to say because I almost feel the same way. 'I'm so excited about tomorrow. I hope your mum does not mind us coming?' he asks.

'Oh no, in fact, she is pleased. We will have company, and you will meet my friend too, Charlotte.'

'I'm excited and can hardly wait. Pearl is excited too,' he says next.

'That makes three of us,' I say, sounding enthusiastic.

'Okay, see you tomorrow at six then. Goodnight, Yasmine.'

'Night, Jace,' I say calmly and hang up.

I feel exhilarated. The glee in my heart knows no bounds. Mum only glares at me and shakes her head. She must think her daughter is going insane.

After dinner, I go upstairs, take a shower and lay down to sleep. Feeling anxious about Thanksgiving dinner, I turn on my iPod to help me unwind. I absorb the lyrics to Westlife's "That's Where You Find Love", and let the sound lull me to sleep…

My alarm rings loudly, waking me up from my deep slumber. It's Thanksgiving! My mum says we always have to celebrate it because we have loads of things to be grateful for, and she is right to reflect on everything that has happened to us. We have to be thankful for our family, and my definition of family is just Mum and myself. I turn on my CD player and start combing through my assortment of CDs, searching for the perfect piece to help me begin the day. I settle on Celine Dion's "A New Day" album. My love for Celine's vocals is mad; the way one line of her lyrics rolls into the next one, without going off track, keeping her pitch. There is nothing not to love about her songs. The first track, "I'm Alive," starts playing, and I get up, do some stretching exercises and walk to the bathroom. I splash some water on my face, run down to the kitchen, and make myself a cup of strong black espresso. I return to my room to enjoy my espresso and music while getting ready for the day. Boy, it's going to be a long day. *Today is going to be a jean kind of day*, I think to myself. I pick out black jeans and a clean blue top. Blue is one of my favourite colours. I particularly enjoy wearing it because it compliments my blue eyes. I dress up, apply light makeup, pick up my bag, and head to the kitchen. My mum comes down in her robe. Today is one of her favourite days, so I understand the reason for her being overly optimistic.

'Good morning, sweetie,' she says.

'Good morning, Mum. Happy Thanksgiving,' I wish her.

'Happy Thanksgiving, sweetie.' She reaches over to kiss me on my forehead.

I reminisce back to when I was a kid. Thanksgiving used to be special. Mum and Dad used to invite people over for Thanksgiving dinner and cooked different delicacies. My mum loved cooking, so occasionally, she went the extra mile and made about nine dishes for the guests. It was such an upbeat ambience. Unlike now, my mum only cooks three different dishes; roasted turkey, the tender bean casserole, which is my all-time favourite because I only get to eat it once a year, and mashed yams. My mum has her recipes for these dishes, which she acquired from her mother. I have to help in the kitchen because I can't make it half as good as she does. This morning, Mum is making pancakes. I quickly steal one from the plate, and she threatens to break my bones if I grab another one, so I patiently wait for her to finish making them.

'I'll not be going to work with you today. I'll brief you on what to do. You are the chief today,' Mum says.

'Does that mean I can fire Jean?' I ask with a deadpan voice. Jean has an annoying habit of gawking at me at work. He stares so often that I can't help but notice. It's not a serious issue, simply a vexing situation.

'You can't sack people because they find you attractive, Bebe.'

'The way he stares at me creeps me out. That is not attraction if you ask me.'

My mother rolls her eyes. She feels I'm overly dramatic with the Jean situation.

'By the way, you don't have the authorisation to sack anybody, and please come back early to assist me in preparing dinner.'

'Yes, ma'am.' I do a mock salute.

'Take the car, but make sure you don't scrape it, or

your next pay goes towards it.' I do another mock salute.

When she finally makes the pancakes, I devour them and leave for work. I go about my business of the day. My heart is singing in delight about the evening. I'm using all my willpower to concentrate at work. I do everything my mum asked me to do for her, discharge everyone by 3pm and head home.

When I get home, the turkey is already baking in the oven, and it smells heavenly.

'Great job you are doing here, Mum. I feel like eating the house.' I go to where she is and peck her on the cheek.

'Welcome, sweetheart. How was work today?'

'For starters, I did not fire Jean.' I start towards my room.

She laughs.

'I'm glad you are learning to deal with life situations,' she shouts after me.

I change out of my clothes. As I sprint back downstairs to help Mum get the meal ready, the doorbell buzzes.

'Charlotte is here,' I announce.

'Is she here?' she immediately whispers as she comes in.

'Yes, she has stashed herself in my bathroom,' I hiss.

'You are never serious,' she says and hugs me.

'And you are never early for anything. How come you are early today?' I shoot back.

She scorns me and goes to the kitchen to greet my mum.

'Hi, Mrs B, Happy Thanksgiving.' They hug, and she kisses my mum on both cheeks. 'I brought a present. I'm French, and we don't celebrate Thanksgiving, but no one should miss this sweet-smelling soul food,' she says while bringing out a neatly wrapped package from her handbag, which she hands to my mum.

'That's so sweet and considerate of you, Charlotte. Thank you,' Mum says, and she unwraps it. It's a bottle of Bordeaux wine. I take it from Mum and place it in the refrigerator.

'Should chill in time for dinner,' I say and mouth a thank you to Charlotte. She is such a gem. She joins us in preparing dinner. We decided not to dress up until the food is ready. Mum sets the plates on the dining table and garnishes them, making the table very drool worthy.

I take a bath and get into my black satin dress with tiny straps. It has pleatings bunched together on one side and a low-cut neckline, but not too low. It's tight at the midriff and shows off my slender waist well. I put on a single string of white pearls around my collar, with matching earrings; a legacy from Maman from long ago. I'll always treasure them. I pick out my favourite black heels and put them on, striding in front of the mirror to look at myself, wondering what Jace will say when he sees me.

'Simple and chic,' Charlotte announces from behind me.

I beam, satisfied with my look. I apply a little gloss on my lips and black eyeliner on my eyelids for my eyes to pop out.

'Oh, my! You are going to have him going nuts,' Charlotte compliments again.

'I'm going to go nuts with your endless compliments,' I moan, and she laughs wickedly.

'In that case, I'm going to continue doing it all night, baby,' she replies.

I can only shake my head and hope she does not carry out her threat. I walk downstairs to show Mum my dress, stop in front of her and spin around so she can have a pleasant view.

'You look lovely, my dear. As always.'

'You look dashing too, Mum. Strangers wouldn't believe you are my mother. They would assume we're sisters.'

I head toward the refrigerator and pull out the wine Charlotte brought earlier. The drink is chilled now. Charlotte comes down wearing a strapless green dress that ends just above her knee. Her hair is in a bun, and she has minimal makeup on.

'Looking like a bag of money, Charlotte,' I say, and she

does a little waltz. Trust her to revel in extol.

Suddenly, the doorbell rings.

'That should be them,' I say, rushing to open the door for them.

I fix my dress and spread some gloss on my lips again before I open the door. A lady comes face to face with me. She too sports a simple black dress. I recognise her instantly as the same lady Jace was with during the museum tour. She is a bit shorter than I am and has the same brown eyes as Jace. Her dark hair is neatly curled and pinned atop her head. Some curls escape, framing her heart-shaped face.

'Hello, our pretty tour guide!' she exclaims and waves.

Her voice is velvety and innocent, as if a child is speaking.

'Hello, you must be Jace's sister,' I reply with a smile while still trying to look outside for Jace, since it seems like he is not with her.

'Yes, and you are Yasmine. You told us your name during the museum tour. I have not forgotten. I have heard so much about you,' she replies. Her obvious compliments bring a smile to my face.

'Thank you, and it's so kind of you to remember my name. Where is Jace?' I ask.

'Jace will be here shortly. He had to attend to something,' she says.

'So, he is not coming?' I ask to be sure.

'He wouldn't miss this for the world. He will be here in a few minutes,' Pearl replies with a wide smile in place.

'Oh, I'm sorry, my bad. Please come in,' I say as I move away from the entrance.

'Any idea where he went?' I ask.

'Okay. Jace forgot to get you something, so he went to get you flowers. Don't tell him I told you.'

My heart melts all over again. Jace is just too sweet to be true. Just as I'm thinking about him, there is a soft knock on the door. I don't bother asking who it is; instead, I open it immediately. There he is, in all his handsomeness. His black tuxedo looks like he was born in it and his blonde hair is neatly trimmed. He looks hot. He smiles at me, and my tummy begins that floating action they describe in novels. I think they call them butterflies.

'Hi,' he whispers with a smile.

I return a smile to him as well. I'm stunned by how handsome he looks. How can a man look like he comes out of a magazine every day?

'I got these for you,' he stretches the bouquet of red roses to me, and I don't hesitate to collect it from him. I let the smell transport me to the beautiful corners of my heart, grateful to smell such sweetness.

'They smell very nice. Thank you,' I say.

'I got one for your mum, too. I hope she likes them. I'm nervous,' he says, scratching his neck as he speaks.

'She will love them. Relax, my mum is not a dragon. Take deep breaths and exhale. Mum! Charlotte! They are here!' I shout to inform them of Pearl and Jace's arrival.

'We're coming,' Charlotte answers from the kitchen.

'Please come and sit,' I say to Pearl and Jace, as I usher them into the living room. I'm sure Mum and Charlotte are already setting dinner up. That must be why they are not down yet. Thinking of all that food is making me hungry.

'Hello there!' I hear my mum's pleasant voice say. Even to my ears, her voice is like fine silk. I can never tire of hearing it. 'Oh my! You must be Jace, and you must be Jace's sister. I'm pleased to meet you both.'

'Good evening, Mrs Belmont. I brought these for you,' Jace says, presenting a bouquet of red roses to her.

'Oh, thank you. The roses are fragrant and beautiful. I have not received flowers in ages, and please call me Juliette,' my mother says, grinning from ear to ear.

'You have a lovely place, Juliette,' Pearl says.

'Thank you, dear. I have always believed that less is more, so I like to keep everything simple,' Mum replies, basking in the cascade of compliments.

'I hope I'm not late,' Charlotte says, half running in from the kitchen and almost tripping in her high-heeled sandals. I roll my eyes. She is never punctual.

'Jace, Pearl, meet Charlotte, my friend.'

'Hello Charlotte,' they both say in unison. 'Pleasure

meeting you.'

'I feel like I have seen you somewhere,' Charlotte says to Jace, and Pearl smiles slyly.

I felt the same way the first time I saw him.

'Okay! That is enough introductions. Why don't we eat?' I say.

Pearl rubs her palms together and follows my mum to the dining table. Charlotte squeals with joy and I follow behind Jace closely. Charlotte pulls me back after everyone else has gone to the dining table and whispers harshly.

'You give lousy descriptions. How do you work as a guide? This is a man out of a movie! La Vache!' she exclaims with excitement in her voice.

I can't help but laugh at her palpable excitement. 'They will notice we're not at the table,' I say and push her toward the dining table.

At the table, I sit next to Jace. As I sit, he leans into me and whispers.

'You look stunning.' I blush at the compliment; grateful I had put in a bit of effort to look spectacular for him tonight. I mouth a 'thank you,' and I adjust to my seat. After dishing the food out onto everyone's plates, we all eat. My mum clears her throat. I'm sure she is about to bombard Jace with various questions.

'So, Jace, I hope you are enjoying your holiday, and you too, Pearl?' my mum asks.

'Of course. The tour of this city has been beautiful, and if I'm candid, Yasmine's tour is my all-time favourite,' Pearl says. 'I wanted to thank you for that beautiful tour, but my brother already did that,' she lets out a soft laugh.

'How long do you intend to stay for?' my mum asks again.

'We're still thinking. As you know, it's meant to be a 15 day tour around Europe, but I think I like it here. I want to see more of this beautiful city,' Jace replies. This time, with eyes on me the entire time.

Afterwards, everybody eats a bit seriously. Charlotte and Pearl are getting on well. My mum continues to pipe Jace with all the questions in the world. I continue to eat because I'm famished and don't have any conversation left in me. I need to refuel.

'It's time for a toast!' my mum announces. She opens the bottle of wine Charlotte brought earlier and pours it into five wine glasses on the table, handing each of us a drink. 'This is something Yasmine and I do every year. So, I want you all to make toasts to what you are thankful for. I'll go first,' she says and then smiles. 'I'm thankful for family,' she says.

'I'm thankful for happiness and everything I have in life,' I say after her.

'I'm thankful for my brother,' Pearl says.

'I'm thankful for life and my sister,' Jace says, with a

serious and sad look on his face. The look is only present for a minute before a small smile makes its way to his face.

'I'm thankful for growth,' Charlotte says.

We clink glasses before everyone takes a sip from their glass.

'Thank you all,' my mum says. 'Thank you for coming. Thank you for making this night a special one for Yasmine and me. Let's have some dessert!'

Mum had already prepared a macaron for dessert. Charlotte goes into the kitchen to get dessert while I clear the used dishes on the table. Pearl offers to help, but I tell her not to worry. Jace gets up and starts clearing the table with me. I also tell him not to worry about it, but he does not listen.

'Forgive my manners milady. I forgot to tell you how beautiful you look today,' he says to me on our way to the kitchen.

'You already did, but compliments have killed no one,' I answer, revelling in the attention I'm getting from him. 'You're not looking so bad yourself with that handsome movie star thing that you have going for you.'

'You flatter me too much, milady,' he says, a pool of brown eyes staring into my soul. We return to the dining table.

'Dessert is here,' Charlotte announces as she brings out the macaroons.

After Charlotte dishes out dessert, I pop a macaron into my mouth and close my eyes, savouring the buttercream filling as it melts in my mouth. No one cooks like my mum when she wants to. I look at the time since it's starting to get dark; it's the perfect time for a walk. Whilst clearing up the plates used for dessert, Charlotte corners me.

'Ask him to go on a walk with you so you can have some privacy. Your eyes have barely left each other all evening,' she squeals in an excited voice.

I roll my eyes. 'You are being dramatic. Who will do the dishes?'

'I'll take care of that. You have some fun.'

'Thank you,' I say and then hug her.

I ask, 'Hey Jace, I'm going for a walk. Wanna come?' He doesn't hesitate to join me.

'It's cold out here, isn't it?' I ask.

'Not really. It's just perfect,' he comments.

'Jace? Can I ask you a question?'

'Go on,' he approves.

'Earlier, you said you are thankful for life. You said it with so much seriousness, like a person who has had a close shave with death.'

'I'm fine, Yasmine,' he says, cupping my face in his

hands as he sighs. 'Do you perhaps remember a band, Soft Division?' he asks.

Of course, I remember Soft Division, the band of four. They had their entire album on the billboard for weeks; two albums topped the charts back-to-back.

'I used to be the lead guitarist of Soft Division. However, we got stupid and started using drugs. Peruvian-Albin, meth, everything. It killed my best friend, Aiden. I gave him Peruvian-Albin. He sniffed it and started coughing out blood afterwards. The doctor said he had internal bleeding, so he died. Every day, I blamed myself for letting him sniff it until I went to rehab and had therapy. I wish we had made better decisions. He would be alive now,' he pauses. Tears stream down his face as he speaks. I could only feel for him. I rub his back to comfort him.

'I'm sorry about your friend,' I say to him as he wipes his tears away.

'Your turn,' he says

'My turn what?'

'I want to know everything about you,' he says, and I feel my cheeks flush.

'Okay, I used to live in America with my mum and dad. Just the three of us. My dad lost his job, and life became a living hell for myself and my mum. He abused her emotionally and verbally at first. One day he came home late, drunk as a skunk, and Mum talked to him. He beat her to a pulp and tried to slit her throat. In that moment, I ran to the phone to call 911. I told them everything that had happened. The police arrived a few minutes later, then the ambulance. He didn't slit her throat, but he left bruises on her body. The police arrested my dad. My mum decided not to press charges but divorced him, and we had to move back to France.' My eyes are getting misty.

'I'm so sorry you had to experience something as cruel as that,' he says, his eyes full of empathy.

With my hands in his, he pulls me into a hug. I look up and stare right into his eyes for a moment. This man broke down all the walls I built around myself within such a short time. Everything he says, his steps, and his actions make me fall for him repeatedly. It seems so unreal that I could fall for someone so quickly. I move my face closer to his and then plant a kiss on his lips; our lips move in sync. It's gentle and giving at first. I feel his breath against my face, and the eagerness in his body as his hands move to cup my face. Then it becomes intense as our bodies yearn for one another. I feel sparks all over; I feel butterflies in my tummy. He breaks away first.

'This is not how I want this to be,' he says, rubbing my shoulder as he speaks.

'You have less than 15 days here,' I say, huffing. 'We could make it memorable,' I suggest, biting my lip.

'What are you suggesting?' he asks.

'I want to share my life with you. All my deepest secrets and desires. I want everywhere in Europe to hold a mysterious secret about us,' I explain. He smirks.

'I'm honoured that you want to do this with me,' he says.

He pulls me closer, and I land on his broad chest. We kiss again, this time more intensely than the first. I close my eyes and let him lead me. His hands trace my curves, whilst mine are locked in his hair. Nothing matters at this moment.

'It's late already, Princess. Let's go home,' he whispers against my lips.

I nod, and we head back with our hands intertwined, a look of happiness and contentment on both our faces. We reach home to find my mum worried. She had already become best of friends with Pearl. Charlotte throws me a wink.

'We should get going, Jace. I feel sleepy already,' Pearl yawns.

Jace picks up his jacket from the coat stand. They both thank my mum for a beautiful evening.

'Goodnight, Charlotte. It was nice meeting you,' he says.

'Goodnight, Jace. The pleasure is all mine,' Charlotte replies.

Outside, he hugs me. I could not have felt better at that

moment. He then plants a kiss on my forehead.

'Ugh! Come on, love birds. I need my beauty sleep!' Pearl interrupts, making him burst into laughter.

'I can drop you off at your hotel,' I offer.

'No,' he and Pearl say in unison.

'We will take a cab. Go on in,' Pearl says this time around.

I hug her, bid them goodnight again, and walk back into the house. My mum is preparing to retire for the night.

'I have been waiting for you. I'm going to get a much-needed rest,' Mum says.

'Goodnight, Mum.' I go over to her and plant a kiss on her cheek.

'Goodnight, Charlotte,' my mum shouts. 'And thank you for your help today.'

'Goodnight, Mrs B.'

'How was your walk?' Charlotte asks while we clean up.

'Well, it went better than I expected,' I reply, smiling as I reminisce about what happened.

'You will give me all the dirty details later,' she says with a girlish giggle.

That kiss felt like my first kiss. Jace's lips tasted like heaven. I can't wait to feel them on mine again. He makes me feel so safe, as if I have known him my whole life. I love the feeling he gives me when I'm with him. I can't believe

I'm this smitten by a person I just met. Charlotte and I go upstairs to my room. I don't want to wash the night's event off me yet, so I ask Charlotte to use the bathroom first.

'Now, you are ridiculous,' I say to myself.

I smile as I think about the crazy moment we shared while we were on our walk. Maybe I have found love. Perhaps I'm not destined for a life of heartbreak from men. I give Charlotte the details of my walk much later, but I leave out the part about his best friend and past life. Everything seems scary. Sharing it feels like a violation of our budding love. I love how he confided in me with his problems. I also understand that there are many things that we don't know about each other, but we have time, don't we? Maybe Jace is not like the other guys; perhaps he is not like Andrew. Jace makes me want to try new things. Things I would never try with anyone else. And now? I want every place in Europe to hold a mysterious secret about us.

Chapter Three
Jace Tanner

I've come to realise that Paris is not a particularly quiet city. Well, that's not surprising with the number of people who live here and visit. My hotel room, however, is different. It must have soundproof walls or something, because it's remarkably silent in here. The tour company booked these rooms as part of our travel package, and I can say that I'm pleased with their arrangements. It's mostly calm in the mornings, and today is no exception. The only difference today is that the air feels strung with optimism. I wake up with a spring in my step and a smile on my lips, and I know just the reason for that. I'm meeting Yasmine today, and that's the only reason I need to feel upbeat. Being with her brightens me up in a way I never dreamt possible. Yes, I know being this drawn towards someone I barely know is not healthy, but I'm looking for happiness, and it seems I might discover it here. A knock on the door brings me out of my reverie.

'Well, hello, superstar,' Pearl beams at me from the door. 'You look…' she says, struggling to find a word. I tilt my head in anticipation of what adjective Pearl is about to use. She is full of surprises, after all. 'You look very excited,' she finally completes. I can't help but agree with her. I feel cheerful, and I wish to feel this way for as long as possible.

'Good morning to you too, Pearl,' I jokingly reply to her, to which she waves me off.

'Oh please. When did you start caring about mornings?' She knows I'm not a morning guy.

'Well, Paris mornings are exquisite,' I counter defensively.

'Oh, really?' she snorts. 'Is that a fact… or?' she drags out.

I realise what's coming next and start laughing.

'Does it have anything to do with a gorgeous tour guide who has dark hair and blue eyes that drive your heart into a gallop, your eyes to twinkle, makes you sing for joy and…'

'Okay, that's it,' I cut her off as soon as I sense an unmanly blush forming on my cheeks.

She laughs loudly and hysterically as I shove her out of my room.

'Get your ass out of here,' I say in between grunts as I attempt to chase her out.

She finally budges and turns around while flicking her hair.

'She has stars when looking at you… just so you know,' she says, while going back to her room.

I grin, and I'm glad she doesn't see it. Just when I assume she is gone, I hear her yell, 'I call dibs on being a bridesmaid.'

A boisterous laugh escapes me as she finally closes the door. She's such an affable character. I love her so much, and I'll forever be grateful to her for being there in my life. I get a tight feeling in my chest, but it's not a terrible feeling. I feel reminiscent, and I know just what I need now. Standing up from the bed, I reach for my travelling bag, which I have refused to unpack, and open a small, frequently overlooked zip. I find what I'm searching for; all the CDs we created as Soft Division. We may have publicly released just two albums, but we loved all four of our mix tapes. Some songs remained unreleased because our sponsors informed us that their content wasn't profitable enough, so we combined them into mix tapes. I pull out one of my favourite CDs, "Wild Side." One of our first albums. Luckily for me, the room came equipped with a CD player, so I turn it on and slot in the CD. "Wild Intentions" starts to play, and I feel joy growing in my heart as happy memories of our beginnings as a boy band swarm to the surface of my mind. This song blew Soft Division and catapulted Aiden, Cross, Russ, and me to instant stardom for the second time. It holds a special place in my heart.

When the chorus plays, I sing along and play air guitar, mimicking the way I played it in the song.

'*You may not believe me,*
But I hope one day you will,
My intentions for you are good,
Although they are not holy,

But rather as wild as sin,
Cos, baby, wild intentions are all I have for you.'

We composed the song in our dorm room, and it came to be the song that got people hooked on our album. As the second verse plays and I get ready to sing along, I hear rapid taps on my door, and Pearl bursts in almost instantaneously. She has her phone in one hand and signals for me to kill the music.

'Oh my God, Jace. It's Russ.'

As she mentions Russ, I dash to the phone, grab it from her and place it upon my ear. My heart is thumping hard. I have been so concerned about Russ and Cross, and I've been unable to get a hold of them.

'God, please, let them be all right,' I say in a silent prayer.

'Hello, Jace,' comes the all too familiar voice of Russ.

'Russ! Man, I've been trying…' I start to say, but I'm cut off when he continues to speak. I can hear the panic in his voice.

'Man, I need your help. Cross is dying.' He drops it on me like an A-Bomb.

I feel my mouth turn dry, and my head spins.

'What? What is happening?' I choke out.

'He overdosed, bro,' he yells out, and tears start flooding my eyes. 'He's in the hospital, right… in critical condition, and the experts are saying I have to wait hours before they can find out if he's going to make it or not,' Russ continues as I feel chills down my spine. 'I'm in over my head, man.' Acute dread and sorrow fill his voice as he says this, and I finally wake up from my shock-induced state.

'Text me the address, and I'll be there as soon as possible.' Pearl rushes to where my clothes are and starts stuffing them in my travelling bag. 'I'll be there, alright, man?'

When Russ assures me he understands, I end the call and run to pack my luggage.

'I'll go pack mine and book the closest flight home.' Pearl runs to her room.

I finish packing my clothes before sitting down on the bed with my head on my palms. I immediately jump up, realising that there's no time to mope around now. I clear out my things from the bathroom and decide to call Yasmine, as I don't want her to think I stood her up. Gingerly scrolling through my contact list, I spot her number and press call. As it rings, I try to think of what to say to her. My head is crammed with images of me rushing Aiden to the emergency room, waiting with trepidation for the doctors and medics to give me the news. When I was informed that he was dead, I recall walking into the hospital room he was in, seeing his face, and feeling my world crashing down around me. It terrifies me that Cross might be in the same situation right now.

'Why did we start all this?' I whine.

When she picks up, and I hear her preppy voice, my mood spirals downward.

'Hello, Jace. How are you doing?' she asks.

'Hi, Yasmine. I'm good.' I bite out. 'Something has come up, and that's why I'm calling you.'

I can hear the flatness in my voice and wonder just how much of it she hears. When she remains quiet, I continue, 'One of my close friends and a fellow band member is in serious trouble. He needs my attention, so I have to go back to America immediately.' I don't know why I don't tell her about his hospitalisation, but I decide to hold that piece of information back for a reason.

'Oh,' she says, 'I'm sorry to hear that. Are you coming back?'

'I don't know. I'll let you know if I do,' I say and drop the call immediately. 'Why was I so rude and curt to her?' I groan. 'She is going to hate me, and it's all my fault.'

When Pearl comes back in, she finds me sitting on the bed with my phone in my right hand and my head nestled in my left palm.

'Alright, I have booked a flight, and it's leaving in an hour. Let's get a move on.'

I stand up and follow her out the door and out of Europe.

Russ Adams, the bassist of Soft Division, was born into a preppy, wealthy family. When we met him in college, he didn't even look like the type of person who would hang out with us. It looked like Russ belonged in debate clubs and student union meetings with his well-ironed shirts and fitted trousers. It shocked us when he came up to us on the last day of freshman week, while we were gulping down some sodas.

'Hi, guys!'

'What's up, Professor?' Aiden chuckles

'Aiden!' I nudge him discreetly before turning to the boy. 'Hey man, what's up?'

'Cool,' he says, tightening his hands on the textbooks he was holding. 'I… Erm… I heard you guys sing yesterday in your dorm room, and it was terrific.'

'You're in our dorm?' Aiden asked almost simultaneously as I said, 'Thanks, man.'

'Yes, I'm in your dorm, just a few rooms away from yours. I was going back to my room when I heard you. I promise it wasn't deliberate,' Russ spurted out in a rush, looking worried already.

'It's cool, man. Thanks,' Aiden said, which appeared to calm his nerves.

What he said next was the last thing we expected to hear from him.

'I want to join your group.'

Aiden spits out his drink in surprise and I averted my foot from the direction of his drink-splatter while staring at the boy with a dumbfounded face.

'Okay, look, man, we don't need cymbal players or violin players either,' Aiden laughed.

'Man, what's your name?' I asked.

His blossoming courage replaced the nervousness. 'My name is Russ, Russ Adams, and I don't play the cymbal or violin. Rather, I'm a bassist, and I'm quite good at it.'

Aiden and I exchanged surprised looks while we mulled over it. Aiden nodded, so I turned back to Russ and extended my hand for a shake.

'Of course, man. Let's meet up tomorrow morning.'

It was a partnership that turned into a brotherhood. We had the idea of starting a band, but something always seemed missing. When we put out a notice of auditions for a new band member, a few people came: singers, guitarists, and dancers. I don't know where singers got the idea from, but no one gave us the spark we were searching for. The last guy introduced himself as Cross and said he played the drums. When he played the drums along with a CD we recorded, we knew we had found precisely what we were searching for. He gave our songs a new life, and hope surged in our hearts for a future as celebrities. When we thanked everyone else and left, we conversed with him and dug deeper. Cross Stephen was a native of the town and attended college on a full-ride scholarship. He and his mum lived in a trailer park, and he was going into his second year. He had been drumming at his church since he was twelve. We gave him an official invitation to join our budding group, and he gladly accepted. And just like that, Soft Division was born. It seems just like yesterday.

Following the directions Russ sent is very easy. The hard part is gathering the courage to walk into the hospital. Hours upon hours of plane rides had not required this much courage. Now we were finally here. I walk into the hospital with Pearl right behind me. We make inquiries at the reception desk about the whereabouts of Russ and Cross, who direct us to a room down the hallway. When we get closer to the room, the first thing I see is the huddled frame of Russ on a waiting chair. I move closer to him, but he doesn't notice as he's holding his head in his hands with his eyes squeezed shut. I can see worry written all over him, so I gently tap on his shoulder. When he opens his eyes to see me, he jumps to his feet and hugs me hard.

'Jace, man, you're here.'

'I'm here, Russ. I'm here.'

I see as the worry reduces in his expression, and I know it's because he has found someone else to share it with.

Pearl moves in from behind me to give him a hug.

'How are you doing, Russ? Wait, that was a stupid question,' she corrects herself, and this makes Russ crack out a smile.

'I have been better, Pearl,' he replies.

When his eyes meet mine, a shared look of deep guilt and regret settles into us. Taking his hands in hers, Pearl squeezes it reassuringly before letting go, and we all sit down. Pearl and I take seats right next to him.

'How is Cross doing?' I ask, dreading the answer.

'I don't know, man. The doctor came out and told me his condition was still critical and advised me to go get food or rest as it might take some time before we receive a definite answer,' Russ replies while scratching his head, 'But man, I can't leave him here. I need to know what's up before I can relax enough to eat or take a fucking shower.'

'Okay, how about I grab you some coffee and doughnuts from the shop across the street?' Pearl says as she stands up. When Russ moves to decline her offer, she adds, 'And no, I wasn't offering. I was telling you.'

She leaves, and Russ smiles again. 'I missed her bossiness.'

We sit in silence for a while until I look over at him and see tears streaming down his face.

'Why did we start this?' I hear him say, and all the guilt, anger, and frustration I have been feeling for the past year resurfaces, making me feel like hitting a punching bag or putting my fists through a wall. 'Why did we get into this in the first place?' he continues, with his pitch rising with every word. 'We can't say that nobody told us about the consequences because we knew all about it and still stupidly pushed on.'

'Russ, we were stupid, and our stupidity has taken a life, our careers, and our happiness,' I reply softly. 'This is exactly how Aiden was,' I continue, remembering how I sat in almost the same place, feeling this same way and hating myself. 'God, please,' I murmur.

When Russ has calmed down, we sit quietly for a few minutes before he speaks again.

'Do you know why you couldn't get hold of us for a while?' he asks, and I shake my head. 'When Cross called to inform me of the call he got from you, I quickly got dressed and made my way to the hospital. At the hospital's entrance, I met Cross, and we walked in together. We got to the hallway leading to the waiting room, but we couldn't find you. When we asked a nurse, she told us you were in the doctor's office. We had just got there when you rushed out the door in the opposite direction and ran towards the hospital rooms, but we were some distance away, and you couldn't see us. The doctor was coming out of his office and by then, you had disappeared round the corner. We then introduced ourselves to him as your brothers. We asked why you were running, and he gave us the breaking news...' he pauses before continuing. 'Man, I don't know what happened next. My mind blanked out on me, and the doctor's voice sounded like something in the background. I felt horror dawn on me, and the hospital suddenly felt suffocating. I needed to breathe, so I rushed out with Cross at my heels. When my thoughts returned, I felt so much pain and guilt. We should have saved him. We should have been there to save him, and I couldn't face you or anyone else. I just needed to leave, so I did. I booked a flight back home, where my parents treated me like the prodigal son. You know they never supported my career in music. I changed numbers to disconnect from my old life, but kept Cross's number and kept in touch with him. My parents later encouraged me to go to rehab to free myself of this addiction. By then, Cross's addiction was ten times worse. The only drug he didn't take was meth. Nothing else was off-limits. Injections, heroin, more and more cocaine, pills, alcohol, crack cocaine, Valium, Xanax, codeine, you name it.'

The more drugs he lists, the more I feel like throwing up.

He continues, 'We got ourselves into rehab with the encouragement of our families. Jace, I got better, but Cross couldn't finish it. He dropped out early in the program and went right back to drugs. When I got out, I found out that his addiction had got worse, and yesterday, he overdosed on cocaine. I'm so sorry for bailing on you and Pearl at a moment that was traumatising us all. I know you needed me more then, and I needed you too, but guilt didn't allow me to think straight. Please forgive me.'

'Russ, I understand. I hold no grudges against you. Your welfare had me worried. You are friends turned brothers, and we were all overcome with grief.' The more I speak, the more relaxed he looks, and I realise he was worried that I hated him.

My mind is reeling with information. I'm still contemplating what to say when Pearl returns with cups of coffee and a pack of doughnuts. Both Russ and I have no appetite, so Pearl grabs a doughnut and a cup of coffee and settles back down in her chair to pick at it. Russ turns to Pearl and tells her what he told me, asking for forgiveness. She squeezes his hand before they both turn to sit in their seats. The doctor returns, and we all jump to our feet with bated breaths.

'Hello everyone. Your friend is out of the danger zone, but he can't leave the hospital just yet,' he tells us, and we collectively release our breath.

The doctor tells us we may see him, but he won't talk to us because of the sedative that was just administered to him. We still insist, so we're led to his ward. When I set my eyes on Cross, a feeling of Déjà vu takes root in my memory.

The only difference now is that he's alive, and I was only allowed to see Aiden when he was dead. Russ and I move to stand on either side of his bed and look down at his pale form clothed in a shapeless hospital gown. Pearl stands at the doorway to give us privacy. Jace, Aiden, Cross, and Russ, four friends turned brothers. We've been through so much together, and our future was always bright. It sucks to realise that what we saw as secondary could cause so much damage to us. I can't say a thing as we stand around Cross. We stand there for several long minutes and hold his hands until the nurse comes in to tell us it's time to go. Coming out of the room, Pearl and I take turns hugging Russ before we all head to our different homes to eat and freshen up. Now that we're assured of his survival, hunger has arrived in full force, and I desperately need to sleep.

After taking a shower and eating, I lie down on the bed and debate calling Yasmine. I try her number, but no one picks up.

'Damn. Maybe she's furious at my abrupt departure.'

I lay there until sleep overpowers me, only to wake up to the sight of a rapidly darkening sky seen through my bedroom window.

'I can't believe I slept through the day. Now, what will

I do tonight?'

I decide to search for Pearl. I can't find her, so I go into the kitchen and see a note on the counter. *I'm going to the supermarket to get food and cleaning materials. See you soon. Love, Pearl.* Sighing, I place the note back on the counter and contemplate what to do now that Pearl is not here.

Yasmine Belmont

My mum's worried voice breaks through the silent room. 'Yasmine, what happened? Why are you looking so sad?'

Holding back the tears that are threatening to escape my eyes, I shake my head.

'Nothing, Mama, I'm fine. Just a headache,' I lie.

My mum tsks at me, seeing through my lies effortlessly.

'Oh, honey, you are on the verge of tears. Please talk to me.'

She sits down on my bed next to me, and pulls my hands into her lap. Unable to resist, I tell her everything.

'Mum, yesterday was perfectly fine. He left after saying goodnight, and we talked on the phone. Just for him to call this morning and sound completely different from how he used to. He's gone back to America, Mum.'

I was crying by the time I finished. My mum didn't need to ask who "he" was. She just knew.

'Shhh, baby girl. He has his reasons for going back. Even if he doesn't, it doesn't matter. The fact that you feel hurt does not diminish your importance, and there should be no one capable of messing with your happiness.'

Absorbing my mum's words, I wipe my tears and nod. 'Okay, Mum.'

'Now you listen,' she says, 'whether he comes back or not, bear in mind that your feelings mean a lot to me, and no one should have the audacity to mess with them. Don't let anyone tell you that you're overreacting, okay?'

I nod and hug her, and she kisses my head.

'Come eat something.' She leaves my room for the kitchen, I presume.

I stand up, wipe my eyes, and straighten my clothes before moving to the kitchen. When I sit down on a chair around the counter, Mum slides a plate of sandwiches over to me.

I am just taking my first bite when she blurts out, 'We're pressing charges against Monsieur Martin.'

'What? Mum!' I exclaim.

'He tried to molest you, Yasmine. He's not getting off scot-free. Nobody has the right to do that to anyone and roam free as if nothing ever transpired,' she calmly states, 'and when the police went to his workplace to talk to him, his boss was there. She said people like him slander the institute's impeccable name, and she sacked him,' she finishes with a smirk.

'Yes, that makes sense,' I agree before adding, 'I have a group of tourists wanting to go sightseeing today, so I'll just finish up and take off.'

When I finish eating, I go to my room to get dressed. Mum's words have renewed my strength, and all my tears are dried up.

After the tour ends, I get home from work and start fixing dinner for Mum and myself while charging my phone. I'm in the kitchen making a salad when I hear my phone ringing. I make my way to my phone, only to see that there is a missed call from Jace. After standing there for several minutes debating to do, I decide to ignore the call as I don't feel like talking to "Monsieur Cheeky."

After several hours of lazing around and doing nothing with my mind constantly calling, I finally decided to buzz Jace, and he picks up on the first ring.

'Hello, Yasmine.'

'Hello, Jace. How are you doing?'

After a pause, he replies, 'I'm okay. I'm sorry for

leaving like that.'

'Can you tell me the real reason why you had to leave? Is there someone you are seeing back home?' I ask

'No, I can't. And no, I'm not seeing anyone,' he says, and I feel anger bubbling up inside of me.

I'm not sure I believe the reason he gave me before about his band member being in serious trouble.

'Then why are you calling?'

'Yasmine, I'm exhausted and just wanted to check on you.'

'I don't need you to check on me, Jace. I'm fine. If you can't be honest with me about why you left Paris so suddenly, then I have nothing to say to you.'

'I'm sorry, Yasmine. I guess I'll talk to you later,' he says and ends the call.

To say I'm surprised is a gross understatement. Even though I think Jace is different than others, I have been bluffed one too many times by countless boys in the past. Hence, I was unable to allow myself to be taken for a ride again. I really hope that Jace is telling the truth.

'Aargh,' I scream into the empty room.

Jace Tanner

I can't tell her. I just can't. It would betray Cross's trust, and also, it's his private matter, and I don't feel comfortable sharing it with someone who is not in the band. Also, I'm very embarrassed. What happened to Cross could have just as easily happened to me, and I don't want her to think that I might be the next crew member to have an overdose. I don't even know how I'm going to get her to forgive me or if she'll agree to meet up with me ever again. My prayer right now is that Cross makes a full recovery and that the press doesn't get wind of this because they are brutal and uncaring. Tired of all the conflicting thoughts in my mind, I go to sleep.

The following morning, Pearl and I go to the hospital to check on Cross. We meet Russ there, and together we go in. He is awake and looks happy to see us.

'Hey guys,' he says. He looks tired and pale, but he's alive, and that's what matters.

After we all say our greetings, the doctor comes in to examine him. 'He'll be okay to be discharged in a few days. When he's going, I'll give him a list of medication to be taken daily.'

We all agree, and he finishes up, then leaves. When Cross finishes his breakfast, Pearl looks at me before she speaks.

'Cross, what do you think about checking into a rehabilitation centre?'

'No,' he looks up from the hospital gown. A vain man, he is, 'I've already been there, but it didn't work.'

'You know you're lying, Cross,' Russ interjects. 'You left the program after staying for two weeks.'

'How is it supposed to work if you don't work on it?' I add.

Cross's eyes move across our faces, searching for something before settling on mine. He stares hard at me for several long seconds. In my mind, I'm praying he accepts, as one can't force a grown adult into rehab, and I desperately want him to live. The desperation must have seeped into my features because his jaw tightens.

'Alright, I'll go.' He seems like he is gathering his courage.

'Are you sure?' I ask.

'Yes,' he nods more firmly, 'I want to get better. I'm just scared I'll fail again.'

'We will all be right behind you,' Pearl says. 'We're your family and your well-being is our priority.'

His acceptance brings me relief like nothing else, and I feel weak.

'Okay. I'll start making arrangements with the rehab centre I spent time at,' I say. 'They are brilliant at what they do and will take good care of you.'

I move out of the room with Pearl, and we start making calls.

After a few days, just like the doctor said, Cross is discharged, and we take him home to get his bags before moving him to the rehab centre. The people I know say their hellos and inquire about my well-being. We make small talk for a while until it's time to check Cross in. He looks nervous, like someone about to embark on a life-changing journey and wondering if they'll be able to overcome all the temptations. I move to him and clap him on the shoulder before pulling him into a hug. Pearl and Russ say their goodbyes, too, and the staff take him away. It's time to leave, so we make our way back to our homes. Is this how we're going to live our entire lives, with one deathly experience after another? We've lost Aiden, we've lost our music, and we almost lost Cross. All because of our mistakes.

I've spent days cooped up in the house, and I'm craving the outside. Perhaps I should go for a run or grab a coffee just to feel the sun on my skin. I get dressed and go to Pearl's room to let her know I'm going out. I plug in my Walkman and start with a slow jog. Making my way past people, I increase my speed and it doesn't take me long for me to reach a fast-paced, steady jog. After half an hour, I get tired and sit on a park bench to catch my breath and have some water. After relaxing and admiring the scenery, I start back home. I stride and eventually transition into a jog. After running for about ten minutes, I come to a street with some people and lots of shrubs. Suddenly, I'm surrounded by four reporters who jump out of the bushes. Before I understand what's happening, I'm barraged with questions from all angles as microphones and cameras are pointed at me.

'Jace, is it true that Cross has died from an overdose?'

'Can you confirm if Cross is dead?'

'Is it true that you're still doing drugs?'

'Was your rehab not useful at all?'

'Mr Tanner, please answer.'

'Has Russ overdosed too?'

I force my way through them, saying, 'No comments, no comments, please.'

I try to go around them, but they block my path and continue throwing questions at me, all the while I'm thinking, *Who leaked Cross's overdose issue?*

One reporter says, 'Drugs have taken your entire lives away from you, and you're still on them. Why?'

Getting angry, I reply, 'Get away from me. You don't know a thing about what we're going through.' Why are these gossip columnists always sneaking up on me?

Another reporter, a bald and round-bellied one, apparently getting delighted at my anger quips, 'Aiden died. Who is next to die in your little group? It seems you all didn't learn your lesson with him.'

Furious, I push him back and make my way through the space created by my shove.

'Shut your damn mouth, you fool.'

Pushing back the nasty reporter and creating space to move caused the reporter's camera to fall, which is most likely damaged.

'Hey, punk, you have to pay for this.' The reporter makes a grab at me.

I make a run for it and don't stop until I have got to the house and slammed the door shut.

Pearl must have heard me slam the front door as she rushes out from her room into the hallway.

'Jace,' she rushes forward, 'What happened? Why are you looking so rattled?'

My mind is too preoccupied to answer her. Why would that fat, bald fucker say such a thing? Why would he say something like that about Aiden? It's not fair. What happened was a mistake. Why did the reporter say all those things? Has he no conscience? Has he no feelings?

It's not fair. Pearl is still waiting for an answer.

'I broke a reporter's camera.'

She looks shocked and at a loss for words. 'Alright, why don't you tell me everything?'

We sit down at the dining table, and I relate all that happened to her. She doesn't look surprised and responds by saying, 'I can't say I'm surprised in the least. Some reporters act like dogs. They don't care about people's feelings and only care about getting juicy details about people's lives.'

'I know,' I reply. 'It's just that we've always been on their good side, and when everything went down last year, we avoided them and only read about it in the news. This is one of the few times I've been in close contact with them. They trailed me and laid in wait. Apart from being shocked about what he said,' I continue, 'he seemed angry, and I think I might be heading for a lawsuit. We need no more negative press about our band. And more importantly,' I instantly remember something, 'How did he get to know about Cross? Who leaked the information?'

We think long and hard about the issue, but no one comes to mind, so we decide to let it rest for now. I go to my room to rest. I'm not sure I'll be leaving the house any time soon.

Sitting at the dinner table, Pearl asks me, 'How is Yasmine doing?'

Keeping my head down, I reply, 'she's fine,' while guilt kicks me hard.

The truth is, I have not spoken to Yasmine in a long time. It's been more than a week, but I don't feel like I have anything to say to her. I don't want to disappoint her consistently, so I'm just keeping my distance, although it hurts to do so. I feel like I messed up by not telling Yasmine the whole truth about why I had to leave Paris, and I know it's too late to talk about it now. The only way I can resolve the issue is by talking to her face to face, and as Christmas is in a few weeks and travelling is hectic during this time, I can't get back to Paris soon enough.

'I've noticed that you haven't gone out in weeks now. Russ only comes over, and that's all you do. Why don't you complete your tour of Europe?' Pearl says.

I can't stand the guilt that swarms me at the thought of Aiden not enjoying this life and tour. He can't because I gave him the drugs that killed him. I try to think of an argument.

'But it's almost Christmas already, and I don't think we should spend Christmas on the road,' I argue.

'Well, actually,' she says, looking guilty, 'I have plans, and it's going to take a couple of weeks before I'm free, so you're going alone if you want to,' she adds.

'What type of plans do you have?' I suspiciously ask because she looks so guilt-ridden.

'Well, you know this girl I've been seeing for a while now?' I nodded because I'd met Katherine, her girlfriend, a couple of times. She continues, 'She wants to introduce me to her parents, and they suggested I spend some time with them so that they get to know me better, and it's two states away. Please, I really want to go. Katherine's parents have accepted us and just want to get to know me. That's all I could ask for, and I don't want to ruin it,' she pleads.

'Well, you can go, and I'll stay back here. It's okay.'

'No way,' she exclaims, 'you must go. I loved how happy you were when we were there. Go back and complete the tour.'

Well, she has a point. I notice she still looks anxious, and I realise that she's still waiting for me to say that I'm okay with her going to Katherine's home. I smiled at the fact that she thought I would ever deny her this. She gives up so much for me, so what is one Christmas without my sister?

'No need to look so anxious, Pearl. Of course, you can go. I'm ecstatic for you. I know you really like Katherine.'

She jumps up from her chair and gives me a big hug while saying, 'Thank you, thank you, thank you. I promise you'll enjoy it, and even Yasmine will be there.' She wiggles her brows at me, and guilt sinks deeper into my stomach.

After that, we settle down to eat, and when I'm done and about to stand up, she tells me.

'It's 17 days until Christmas. You can use the 15 days for the tour and be back here for Christmas. I'll start arranging your flight to Paris, and then you can take it from there. Just have an enjoyable time in different places, relax and maybe write some songs. I know you haven't written songs for a long time, but you need to. It's what you do best. I also know in my heart that Soft Division is not dead. You all will come back stronger.'

Looking at her, I can tell that she really believes what she is saying. It makes me feel like someone believes in me even when I don't have an iota of belief in myself.

'Okay, Pearl. I'll try to do that,' I assure her.

Well, it seems I'm going back to Paris. I pray luck is on my side when it comes to Yasmine.

When the plane lands at Paris Charles de Gaulle Airport on the ninth of December, I get a taxi that takes me to my hotel, where I take a long shower and then rest. I feel so unsettled and know it's because I'm worried about how Yasmine will react. Gathering my courage, I dial her number. She doesn't pick up on the first two times, so I try it again for the third time, and this time around she picks up.

'Hello,' I rasp out.

'Hello, Jace. To what do I owe this honour?'

'Yasmine, please just listen to me. I'm sincerely sorry for everything, and I owe you at least an explanation of why I rushed home.'

'Oh, you think so?' she retorts. 'Well, I'm not sure I want to hear it anymore. The time for it has elapsed, and since you're no longer coming back to Paris, there's no need for all of this.'

'Actually,' I begin slowly, 'I'm currently in Paris. I just arrived today.'

There is silence on the other end; I think she's trying to process the information.

'Wait, you mean you are in Paris?' she asks.

'Yes, princess. I'm in Paris, and I'm asking you to please give me a chance. I just want to see you and talk to you.'

'Well,' she said, flustered, 'I'm not sure about that. I have work, and the holidays are close by, so you know I'll be busy.'

'I promise not to take too much time,' I reply.

Seeing that she has run out of excuses, she caves in.

'Okay, but just for a short while.'

The feeling of happiness has me doing fist pumps in the air, but I make sure to stay quiet.

'Okay, okay. I'll text you the destination of where

we're meeting,' I say, relieved.

I remember a spot not too far from my hotel. It's quiet yet not lonely, lined with beautifully designed stone seats and many trees to protect one from the sun's rays. I text her the destination and go to bed with a smile on my face, feeling excited about tomorrow. Tomorrow couldn't come soon enough.

The next day, I make my way to our proposed meeting spot half an hour early. Everywhere I look, I see Christmas decorations. Most shops lining the streets are filled with shoppers and people dressed in colourful garbs. Christmas lights are strung all over the roofs, and Christmas decorations peek out from their windows. It makes me crave the warmth and familiarity of my sister, Aiden, Russ, and Cross, and all the holidays we spent together. I'm glad my sister is finally chasing after her own happiness. I sit for about half an hour when a figure approaches my seat. As the figure comes closer, I see it's Yasmine, and my palms sweat. When she's close enough, I stand up. She stops walking a short distance from me, and we just stare at each other. I greedily take in her beautiful appearance. Her eyes look as blue as a clear sky, and her black hair tumbles so beautifully across her shoulders with a few strands resting on her chest. The top button of her dark brown jacket is open, and I can see she is wearing a blue shirt and black jeans. She looks spectacular, and the front of my pants gets tight and uncomfortable. Feeling a throbbing ache beneath my trousers, I discreetly readjust my jacket. I notice as her eyes narrow at my appearance, and I know she observes how I look dull and sad.

'Hey,' she says.

'Hi, Yasmine,' I point towards the chair I had vacated, 'please have a seat.'

She gingerly sits on the chair and pulls her jacket tighter around herself.

'How are you doing?' I try to make small talk.

'I'm good,' she replies with pursed lips. 'How was America?'

I could hear the bite in her tone at the last question.

'America wasn't perfect,' I admit. When she turns to look at me, I decide to bear it all out. 'Actually, Yasmine, I was telling you the truth all along about why I went to America. One of my bandmates was in some serious trouble.'

'Legal trouble?' She asks.

I take out my Blackberry and show her pictures of me with Cross on the hospital bed.

'Health trouble,' I reply. 'You know Soft Division comprises four members, right?' I ask.

'Yes,' she nods. 'You, Aiden, Russ, and Cross,' she mentions, and I'm pleased she knows.

'Cross overdosed.'

'Oh.' She slides over to me and envelopes me in a hug. 'How is he?'

Comforted by her hug, I hug her back. 'Not good. He survived and is now in rehab.'

She slowly pulls away and looks me in the eye before she asks, 'So you were being honest about the reason for your urgent trip to America? You really did get a call from them?' I nod yes, and she holds my hand. 'I didn't know what to believe.'

'Of course you didn't. People rarely believe me, even when I'm honest,' I reply, 'and I'm sorry about being rude earlier.'

'Why didn't you explain everything to me properly? Perhaps I would have been more inclined to believe you,' she inquires.

'I felt like you didn't trust me, which hurt. Especially when I was telling you nothing but the truth,' I admit to her.

She shakes her head at me before reassuring me that such a thing can never happen. When we've sat down for a while, I offer to buy her lunch. It's only noon, but I want to make sure she eats and gets something warm in her tummy. We move to a restaurant close to our sitting spot. Neither of us are dressed appropriately for a fancy place, so we choose a sub-par restaurant and get seated before ordering. When the food arrives, we dig in eagerly. The food looks great and tastes even better. After eating a few spoonfuls of her food, she looks over at my plate before stretching her hand to take a spoonful of mine. I stare at her in surprise as she bursts into laughter,

'What? Your plate looks very appetising.'

I chuckle while slowly shaking my head. Women. When we're both full, we relax and leisurely sip our drinks.

'Why did you decide to come now when Christmas is in two weeks? I thought you said you weren't sure about coming back to Paris,' she inquires.

'I came back mainly to see you, and I also want to complete my tour of Europe.'

'Why did you decide to do it now? Everyone is typically finishing up with work to have the holidays free,' she continues.

'I just want to complete the tour and go home on Christmas day.'

She mulls over it for a moment before speaking.

'That makes sense. Why don't you come over for dinner tonight?'

My heart feels warm at her kind gesture.

'I would love to, but will your mum be okay with that? I know she's not thrilled about me now.'

'Don't worry about that. Mum is just worried about me. Once she sees I'm okay, she'll be okay too.'

After this, we ask for the bill, and I pay before leaving.

I call a cab for her as she moves in for a hug before whispering,

'You still remember the direction to the house, right?'

'Of course,' I reply.

I kiss her forehead and pull her jacket tighter around her before she enters the cab. I close the door behind her and make my way to the hotel.

I intend to walk to Yasmine's house so that I can explore more of my surroundings, so at 3.30pm, I make my way out of the hotel. At five minutes to six, I get there and knock on the door. I have the bottle of wine that I bought in my arms as her mum opens the door.

'Come on in, Jace,' she says in a clipped tone and a tight face.

I walk into the house and hand her the bottle. 'Thank you, ma'am. Please take this.'

She accepts it and thanks me. I follow her to the dining room, where Yasmine is arranging the table, dressed in a silky green gown. It looks great on her and really flatters her skin. Her hair has been curled, and she applied some light makeup. When she sees me walk in, she comes up to hug me and then gives her mum a look I don't understand. Her mum rolls her eyes and gives a brief smile before directing us all to sit.

'Please, let's eat,' she directs.

We all dig in to eat the meal laid out on the table. I'm enjoying a cup of orange juice when the blue-eyed angel's mum speaks, 'So, Jace, Yasmine has told me why you left last time. I just want to tell you something. Next time, please keep her informed. I won't be happy if you do such a thing again. I'm not one to insert myself into her relationships, but I hate seeing her hurt even more. Do you understand?'

'Mum!' Yasmine exclaims.

'Of course, ma'am,' I nod, 'I completely understand, and such a thing will never happen again.'

'Good,' she replies, 'it's good to know we're on the same page,' she finally smiles at me.

We continue eating, and when we finish, I thank Mrs Belmont for the meal.

'Don't thank me, thank Yasmine. She made everything you see here,' she explains.

I turn to see the blushing Yasmine and thank her as well.

'You're welcome, Jace. I'm glad you enjoyed your meal.'

'Why don't you two go into the living area and talk? I'll clean up,' her mum suggests.

'Of course not, Mum. I can't leave all this work for you,' Yasmine argues.

'Honey, you cooked everything yourself, as I was busy

at work. I can clean up,' she counters. 'Now go,' she says, chasing us out of the dining area.

We go to the living room and sit down on the couch. As my green fairy sits, her dress rides up her thighs, and I see ripped tights showing milky skin. She's so beautiful.

'When are you beginning your Europe tour?' she asks suddenly.

'Well, I don't know…' I begin, but she cuts me off.

'…Why don't we start now?' she suggests. 'It's not too late, and I can show you one popular tourist site here. It's not too far if we use a bus.'

'I would like that, but how about your mum?' I ask.

'She'll be okay. The meal is over anyway,' she says, standing up and straightening her gown.

Taking her hand, we walk to see her mum in the kitchen and inform her we're going out.

'I'll bring her back home early, Mrs Belmont,' I announce.

'That's alright. Grab your jacket, sweetie,' she replies.

Yasmine grabs her coat from the coat rack, and I put it on her before we head out. We catch a bus, and Yasmine directs the driver to stop us at the Gare du Nord. When we stop there, I'm awed by the number of people milling around the train station. Yasmine steps right in front of me and clears her throat.

'Hello tourist. I'm your tour guide for the day,' she

says, at which I chuckle. 'We're at The Gare du Nord,' she begins. 'The Gare du Nord station, also known as Paris-Nord, is one of the six large mainline railway station terminals here in Paris. This train station receives trains from different parts of France using the Paris-Lille railway. It also plays host to trains from other countries like Belgium, Germany, the Netherlands, and the United Kingdom. A German-born French architect named Jacques Ignace Hittorff designed it originally. He made use of a neoclassical style of architecture called Beaux-Arts while designing the station, and the station has a U-shaped terminal.'

While she is speaking, I'm listening, but more importantly, I marvel at her beauty and knowledge. She looks radiant as she does what she loves doing, and I'm happy just to listen to her speak.

'It is located in the heart of the 10th arrondissement and a ten minute walk from Gare de l'Est, another prominent train station, although not as prominent as Gare du Nord,' she adds 'In terms of traffic flows and yearly visitors, Gare du Nord is Europe's leading railway station and is the world's 3rd largest in traffic flows, with over 222 million visitors a year. The doors opened on the 20th of June, 1864, and it has undergone some renovations since then,' she completes before coming back to stand at my side. 'It's beautiful in the daytime but looks better at night,' she explains, 'it is rather dangerous at night too.'

I place her hand in my elbow, and we stroll along the Canal Saint-Martin. There are still a few people here despite the time and cold. We keep on moving, and she continues to point out interesting sights and explain them to me. We stroll until we get to the charming Basilique du Sacre-Coeur, which she explains is a Roman Catholic Church and minor basilica dedicated to the Sacred Heart of Jesus. I can't resist stopping to admire and take in the regal building with its imposing structures.

'Strike a pose right there. I want to take a picture of you,' I tell Yasmine.

'Really? Okay.'

She moves to stand in the spot I point at and poses. I move backwards to ensure I get her full frame in the picture and that the Basilique takes up the entire background. The picture I take is good, so I go to take another one.

'Hey, Mister, why don't you stand with her, and I'll take a picture of you both?'

I turn to look at the person, and find a dark-skinned man walking with two small but smiling children. I gladly give him my digital camera and move to stand with Yasmine. After a few clicks, he returns the camera, and we thank him profusely as he leaves with his kids.

'Let's go sit down somewhere,' I say as we head back towards the direction of the Canal Saint-Martin.

We find a wooden bench with intricate designs in a secluded spot. It's situated in a quiet area and gives some privacy from everyone. She sits down, and I park myself very close to her.

'You seem different, Jace. I can't put my finger on how exactly, but you are different,' she states. 'You seem withdrawn.'

Turning around to look at her, I see this beautiful woman that is not obligated to listen to me or tell me anything, but she still is, which shows me that she is genuinely concerned about me.

'Yasmine, when I got that call from Russ, I felt a shift in me.' I decide to tell her everything. 'This whole drug issue started just as an experiment, but it has grown to swallow us whole. I felt smaller than my problems at that instant, and to be honest, I still do. Cross almost died, do you understand? Do you understand that this would have been the second person we would have lost to a drug overdose?'

She moves closer to me and takes my hand in hers.

'No, Jace, I can't say I understand, as that would be a lie, but I do want to share your grief.'

'I feel so fucking terrible, Yasmine. All it needed was for one person among us, one person, to say, guys, let's stop this, and we would have worked together to get better, but instead, we encouraged each other to try it. We felt unstoppable, like a force that was crashing through everywhere. We didn't know that it would only take a single day to turn our worlds upside down. Now we're at the opposite end of where we thought we'd be. It all feels like a dream to us.'

When she squeezes my hands, I feel the emotions choke me up.

'We've all been to rehab, all three of us. Three out of four guys thought that by today, we'd be on billboards everywhere. I feel like a murderer. I feel like I killed Aiden with my own two hands by giving him the coke to sniff. He would have still been alive if not for that,' I conclude, and my thoughts flash to my childhood. 'Growing up in a low-income family as I did,' I explain to her, 'my mum and dad had little. They were great parents and worked hard to provide for us, sometimes doing many menial jobs to make ends meet. One day, Dad stopped to pick Mum up after work as he took that route home, and we had one car. They met with a car crash, and both lost their lives. We were placed into foster care since we had no aunt, uncle, or relative to take care of us. Luckily for us, we were never separated despite the many times we moved around. Aiden's parents were good friends with my parents even before we were born. They had two sons within months of each other, so naturally, we were encouraged to be friends. That's when I got a brother I never had. We applied to the same college after high school, and that's where we met

Russ and Cross. We have always loved making up songs and playing the guitar, so we started a band in college. Pearl lived close to my school and attended a community college, so she became our manager. After months of performing at college parties and empty clubs, we got our lucky break with our first "Wild Off" album. The lead single "Wild Intentions" blew up immediately, and you know the rest.' she nodded at this point. 'We started drugs because we were told it would make us look cooler. You know, give us the bad boys look. First, it was just cigarettes. Then we got into weed and pills. It moved from there to include cocaine, injections, and everything guaranteed to make us high. We were so stupid. We let drugs ruin all our hard work and aspirations.'

'No, Jace, it hasn't ruined it,' she responds.

'What do you mean?'

'What I mean is that it has only delayed your dreams. You can still achieve it all if you want.'

'But,' I hesitate a little, 'there would be no Soft Division without Aiden.'

'You can honour his memory through your music, Jace.'

I keep quiet and envision Aiden's charm, wit, and love for life. He was the band's backbone, and now it seems impossible to think of a Soft Division without Aiden. I rightfully keep quiet and just hold her hand tighter.

'I just wanted to let you know that you have options,' she continues. 'Soft Division was my favourite band, and the songwriting was top-notch. I know it's still in you.'

I bring her hand up to my lips and kiss it to thank her. She seems pensive for a moment before her eyes meet mine.

'I blame myself for my parent's problems,' she blurts out.

'What?' I'm shocked. 'That was not your fault.'

'Listen,' she begins, 'my dad adored me. I was the centre of his world, and he didn't hesitate to let me know that. He told me consistently that everything he did was for me and that he'd always provide for me, even when I earn enough to provide for myself. He did all this and more until he lost his job. We had to downgrade our house and cut out a lot of things we were used to having. He always looked guiltily at me whenever he couldn't get me new shoes or gifts for Christmas or the popular toys all the children had. He started staying away from home, and when he did finally come back, he avoided me. When he started drinking, Mum made excuses for him and said he had a lot of problems and had chosen to indulge in booze as an unhealthy way of avoiding those issues. I thought about his problems and concluded that taking care of me made him drink. The day he almost killed my mum, I was crying so hard as I called the police because although I was a child, I knew he was going to get taken away, but I had to save my mum's life.' She is crying silently now, and I pull her into a hug. 'That's why I think it's all my fault. The thoughts of how to take care of me pushed my old man to drink,' Yasmine says, muffled against my chest.

'Look here, princess,' I guide her face to look at me, 'It's your father's job to take care of you. That's the job of a parent. It's not his job to abuse you or your mum, so don't blame yourself. He did it all by himself and should get all the blame. He first made a promise to your mum to honour and respect her. If he can't abide by that and tries to kill her, what sort of man is he? I'm not disputing that he loves you but always know that you saved your mum's life because he would have killed her. You did a great job and should forever be proud of yourself and not guilty, okay?'

'Okay,' she smiles and brings her face to meet mine.

This kiss differs from the first one. It feels filled with so much understanding of our spirit, loss, fight for survival, and strength. I bring my hand to her neck and take charge of the kiss. Her lips are so soft I could spend forever tasting them. I part her lips with mine and deepen the kiss. She moves closer, and I can feel her breasts straining against my chest. Putting my other hand under her jacket, I pull her as close to me as our sitting position allows. I nibble on her bottom lip, and she opens up for me. My tongue slides into the warmth of her mouth, and I take delight in the moan that escapes her throat. Her tongue tentatively touches mine, and I feel myself groan. The wetness and heat of her mouth have wreaked havoc on my senses, and I don't realise when my hand moves up to her breasts. They feel so soft, even through the layers of clothes she's wearing. I want more. I need more. It's at this moment that I come to the realisation that I'm mauling her in public, and I pull back slowly. She rests her forehead on mine as we both struggle to catch our breaths. Her eyes are still closed, and when she finally opens them, her eyes are clouded with desire. The same thing I know is eminent in mine. I feel stunned all over again at how beautiful she is. Pulling away from me, she straightens in her seat and starts blushing as she looks around us.

'Do you think anyone saw us?' she whispers.

My chest rumbles with laughter. 'That doesn't matter. I'm not afraid to kiss you anywhere.' And I mean every word of what I just said.

Chapter Four
Jace Tanner

Slowly, she brings up her face to meet mine, and I suddenly want to kiss her all over again. My palms move to her cheeks, and she smiles at me. I get the inspiration to ask her what has been bubbling inside me for days now.

'Yasmine, please come on a tour of Europe with me.'

'What?' She sits up straight. 'Are you being serious?'

'Yes, I am.' I take hold of her palms. 'I want to go on a tour of Europe with you. I know it's impromptu, but everything is already booked, and I want to go with you.'

'Jace, I have to work, and besides that, my mum might not be okay with me going outside the country for over two weeks with someone whose entire social information she doesn't know.'

'I forgot about that. I have two train tickets to different tourist sites in Europe. I would have loved to go with you.'

'What countries would you have liked to visit?' she inquires softly.

'Belgium, The Netherlands, Germany, Amsterdam, and other countries with world-known tourist sites.'

I see her eyes shine in excitement. 'Oh, how I would love to see all those places. I know so much about them. I always thought I would book a trip when I'm older.'

'Why don't we talk to your mum?' I suggest. 'I would love to see all these places with you, and I know you want to go.'

She nods, 'Okay. When we're done here, we can ask

her.'

'I heard there's a food market somewhere around here.' I look around, 'do you know where it is?'

'Of course.' She pulls me up from the seat and drags me along with her until we get to what she says is Marché Saint Quentin food market. We find a few open stalls and get some food and drinks, as it's not too late. She converses with the sellers in fluent French, but I only understand a little of what they say. When the stalls start closing, we make our way back to her house. I feel so nervous, and she can sense it.

'There's no need to be so nervous. I have a feeling Mum will be okay with it. I mean, I've always wanted to travel around Europe, and she knows that.'

I nod to assure her I understand, but I'm not sure her mum will be okay with Yasmine going out of the country with someone she barely knows. Her mum opens the door as we get closer, and she ushers us inside. 'Come inside for a minute, Jace, before you go.'

I'm grateful for this and quickly hurry in and out of the cold. I'm taking off my coat when I hear Yasmine and her mum start to speak at once.

'Erm... Mum, I need to as...'

'Yasmine, honey, I need to as...' They both stop talking and burst into laughter.

'You go first, Mum,' Yasmine says.

'Okay, why don't you two sit down?' As we're sitting, she sits opposite us and says, 'Yasmine, would you like to travel with me for these two weeks leading to Christmas?'

'Travel to where, Mum?' Yasmine asks.

'Well, you remember Johnson. We're getting to know each other better, and he got me three tickets for a trip to a private resort on an island. He said one for him, one for me, and one for you,' she says, looking anxious.

Yasmine turns to look at me and smiles before turning back to her mum. 'Actually, Mum, I was about to ask you if I could travel with Jace for 15 days. He has tickets to go on a tour around Europe and asked me to go with him?'

'So, you don't want to come with me?' Her mum asks.

'Mum, you know I honestly like Johnson, but I'm not sure I want to see what you two will be up to on a private island,' Yasmine laughs.

'Well, you're right,' her mum replies, also laughing. 'Don't worry about work when you're gone. When do you two plan to leave? We need to go shopping for more clothes for you.'

'Actually,' Yasmine murmurs, 'we're leaving early tomorrow morning.'

'Tomorrow?' she screams in surprise. 'Why didn't you mention it sooner?'

'I would have done that, ma'am,' I reply, 'but I went back to America urgently and had cancelled the trip. I booked a new one two days ago.'

'Mmm, that is incredibly short notice,' she looks pensively at Yasmine. She turns to me. 'Jace, I'll call you two every day, and if my calls get ignored, I'll get worried. You're a good man, but I have to be extra careful about my daughter.'

'Of course, ma'am. I'll take great care of her and keep in touch with you,' I reply happily.

'Well,' her mum stands up and claps her hands, 'that's all settled then. Pack your bags, baby. Jace, we'll see you tomorrow.'

I stand up and thank her profusely, feeling so much joy in my heart. What a beautiful day it has been.

When I get back to my room, I sit down and go through the itinerary for the trip. There are a lot of places to go to and not enough time to do them all. We might have to squeeze in multiple sites in a day. The first stop is Belgium, where we will visit the world-famous Brussels. I pick up my phone and decide to call Yasmine about tomorrow's plans. When the call goes through, she picks up after a few rings.

'Hi princess. I've got to my room safely and just wanted to let you know about tomorrow's plans,' I state.

'Okay, so what's it going to be like?' she asks.

'Well, our first stop will be in Belgium, where we will go to…' I continue to say when she cuts in excitedly.

'Brussels! Oh my God, I've always wanted to see Brussels, but school and work never gave me the opportunity. Please say it's Brussels we're going to see in Belgium,' she begs, and I laugh at how cute she sounds.

'Yes, it's Brussels,' I finally answer and hear her yell with excitement, 'are you sure you're coming on this trip because of me, or do you just want to go sightseeing?' I ask with a deep belly laugh.

'I don't want to answer that question,' she says in a flat tone before bursting into more laughter.

When our laugh finally calms down, I decide to ask for directions.

'So how do we get to the train station tomorrow, Miss tourist guide?' I tease.

'We'll have to use the Gare du Nord, Mr Wide-eyed Tourist,' she teases back, 'and we'll have to get a cab to take us there. I think it will be better if we book the train tonight.'

We talk for a bit before I decide to let her rest and get ready for tomorrow. I do a little dance in my head. The adventure is about to begin.

Yasmine Belmont

As soon as I press end on the call with Jace, my mum pops her face into my room.

'Honey, I know you are excited and what-not, but we seem to have forgotten something extremely vital.'

'What's that?'

'You're starting school at the beginning of January. I hope this won't distract you.'

Contrary to my mum's thoughts, I haven't forgotten that I'm starting school in January. My acceptance letter to my Master's degree program had come in a short while ago, and classes begin the second week of January. I'm so pumped for it. I'll have ample time to prepare for the start of school, and besides, going around Europe will be a bonus for me.

'Mum, it won't distract me. It will help me see the things I learn about and only see online or visualise. Like my own personal, educational tour, but this time, it will be with someone else.'

'Okay,' she lifts both hands in acceptance, 'I just wanted to make sure.'

She closes the door before opening it and stepping through the threshold. 'Erm,' she clears her throat, 'have you packed everything?'

'I'm still working on that.'

'Don't forget anything important.'

She has this sneaky look on her face, and I hesitantly ask, 'Anything like what?'

'Honey, I know you're not a kid anymore, and I just want to make sure that you're protected.'

I cut in, '…Oh my God, I know I'm older, but I don't think I'll ever be comfortable talking to you about my sex life, and I'm not going to have sex with Jace. We're not that close.'

She sees the embarrassment plain as day on my face before she bursts into laughter.

'You get embarrassed so easily, Yasmine. I'm not asking for all the nitty-gritty details of your love life. I want you to be safe and happy.'

'Okay, Mum, I'm on birth control. I have been on the pill for about a year now.'

'That's my smart baby, but pregnancy is not my only concern, you know.'

'Okay,' I finally realise what she's driving at, 'I won't have sex with anyone without seeing a very recent test result.'

She nods approvingly at me.

'I'm gonna go now,' she whispers dramatically before slowly closing my door.

Exhaling a breath of relief, I continue to get clothes out of my wardrobe and fold them when I remember that

Charlotte doesn't know what's going on. I sit back down on the bed and swipe through my dialled calls until I get to her number. When the call connects, and she picks up, ferocious gum chewing can be heard on the other side of the phone.

'Heavens, Charlotte, are you purposely trying to annoy someone over there?'

'Don't be silly, Yasmine. I just read that chewing gum is a way to exercise your gums,' she laughs.

'Okay, let's say that is correct. Do you have to chew it so loudly?'

We both giggle at this. Charlotte is a character indeed.

'I'm curious as to why you are calling this late.' Charlotte always gets straight to the point.

'Don't freak out, just listen to me,' I start. 'Jace asked me to go on a tour of Europe with him for 15 days, starting tomorrow.'

'Are you being serious?' I hear her spit out something.

'Yes, I am.'

'Well, what did you say? Did you agree?'

'Yes, I did. Look, I know you don't know Jace, but…' I start to say, but she cuts me off.

'Girl, you've been talking to this man for weeks now. He has come to meet your mum twice already based on the information your mum gave me, and we've met his sister. Besides, his personal information is not a secret,' she lists out before dramatically adding, 'I think we know him enough for now.'

I'm so relieved by this. I desperately want my mum and Charlotte to be okay with this trip.

'So, how many places are you going to?'

'He said we're visiting tourist attractions all over Europe for 15 days,' I reply excitedly.

'Bring back souvenirs from EVERYWHERE you go to,' she replies.

'Yes ma'am, of course, ma'am,' I mock salute.

'One more important thing,' she clears her throat, and I have a feeling it's not anything serious.

'I got you some silk lingerie and hot sleepwear. Take them all with...'

I can't believe this. First my mother and now her.

'CHARLOTTE! I'm not going there to have sex with the man. I'm going on a tour. This is winter, and I need nothing silk.'

'Calm your panties, woman. I'm not asking you to wear lingerie at your tourist sites. It's for the room. And I see the way he looks at you. Do you seriously think you won't sleep with him when you're both alone together for more than two days?' She replies triumphantly.

'I'm not doing either of those. Now goodbye. I have to pack my suitcase.'

'Okay, take care of yourself and call me every day,' she

says before we end the call.

I drop my phone on the bed and then resume arranging my suitcase.

Jace Tanner

After booking two cabs to different destinations, I double-check my suitcase for all my clothes and documents. When I've made sure that everything is complete, I take off my clothes and go to bed, feeling excited.

Waking up at 6.30am, I bathe, request breakfast, and get dressed in heavy clothing. Our train ride is at 8.45am, and we don't want to be late for it. I text Yasmine to see if she's awake, and she swiftly replies that she's getting ready. My cab arrives at 8am, and I'm sure Yasmine's cab has also arrived. The taxi drops me off at the Paris Gare du Nord station's entrance, and I wait with my luggage on one of the seats provided there. Sure enough, just a few moments later, Yasmine walks in with her luggage. I catch sight of her first and stand up to meet her. Her brown coat is buttoned up to her throat. Her hair is tied back and covered with a cute little furry beanie and brown boots.

She has a great sense of style, and it pops up without her trying. I lift my hand when she looks in my direction, and she finally sees me and waits for me to approach.

'Hey, beautiful,' I smile, and she grins back at me.

'Hey, hot stuff,' she replies.

I grab hold of her hand, and we walk towards the train platform. The giant clocks around the station tell us it's 8.30am, so we have 15 minutes. Our train will take approximately an hour and thirty minutes. We get our luggage, and I grab hold of her most oversized bag. It's typical of women to pack all their belongings even for a quick trip; it's something Pearl does all the time. As I booked expensive seats, we board the train in the reserved area.

'The train is stopping at Brussels-Midi, one of the most prominent train stations in Belgium,' Yasmine says as we settle down.

'Where would you like to go first when we get there?' I inquire.

We're sitting on opposite seats right next to the window. This gives us a clear view of the outside and gives me a clear picture of her relaxed face. Her eyes light up at my question.

'I want to see Brussels first.'

Laughing at her excitement, I reply, 'Don't you think we should get to our hotel and drop off our luggage first?'

'Silly me,' she remarks. 'I guess I'm too excited about Brussels.'

We make small talk, get snacks and relax. We're both too pumped up to sleep, and even when the conversation lulls, the atmosphere is still very comfortable and calm. Well, as calm as it can be on a train. It doesn't seem long before we arrive in Belgium. The train stops at the Brussels-Midi station, and we alight. We go to the entrance to meet the taxi the hotel has arranged for us. Once the taxi drops us off, we get our keys from the reception and head to our room. We drop our bags and lay down to rest for a bit. She turns to look at me and smiles widely.

'I'm so thrilled right now. Thank you so much.'

'I should be the one thanking you for agreeing to come on this trip with me. I enjoy being around you.'

At my admission, she looks down, but I don't miss the smile on her lips. We hang out for a while before we decide to get a move on. Thanks to the money I paid, the hotel provides taxis to take us anywhere we want to go. When Yasmine realises the service we're getting from the hotel, she gives a weird look.

'What's wrong?' I ask.

'It's nothing serious. Let's talk about it later,' she says, brushing it off.

At this moment, the taxi arrives, and she grabs my elbow and drags me out the door. I look at her and see that she has the biggest grin on her face.

'Come on, let's go,' she says. I find it very amusing. We get in the taxi, and it drives us to Central Brussels.

'Come on, we're here,' Yasmine drags me out of the car before I can thank the driver. Her enthusiasm is addictive, and as she pulls me along, I get as excited as she is.

'Okay, calm down,' I pull her to a stop, 'we would have used a sightseeing bus, but the best ones run for 24 to 48 hours only, and we have little time, so we'll have to use trams or walk to anywhere we want to. When we're going back to the hotel, we'll get a cab.'

'That's quite alright,' she nods.

'Okay,' I rub my hands together, 'where are we going to first?'

The surrounding sight is so captivating and colourful, and I want to immerse myself in everything. Pearl was right. Coming on this trip was exactly what I needed to feel better. We pull out the map and itinerary that we got from the hotel.

'Let's go to the Grand Place.' Yasmine exclaims.

Grand Place it is. As we leisurely make our way in the direction of the Gross Markt, we first make a stop at the Royal Palace.

'Brussels in Belgium is the capital of the European Union. The Royal Place is where the royal family resides, and I've always wanted to see it.'

When we catch sight of the palace, we both stare in awe. Unfortunately, tourists are not allowed inside. It's an imposing structure, with regal columns and guards standing around it. When we're done, we head to the Grand Place.

'Do you know about the market square?' I ask Yasmine.

'Yes, I know a little.'

She then does her thing where she clears her throat and assumes the stance of a tourist guide, which never fails to make me laugh.

'Where we are is the heart of Brussels Old Town. The city's central plaza is one of the best-preserved in Europe. It owes its elegance to its unique architecture and the guild houses,' she points to elegant structures, 'which in Belgium are called Gildehuizen. You can see its intricate designs and ornate roofs all the way from here. I also see lots of rich gold decorations. The Grand Place architects used the Baroque style of architecture, adding some Flemish influences to smoothen it out. Many historical buildings like this have many contrasting architectural designs due to the long construction years, and each time comes with its popular designs. Fortunately, the Grand Place had a short construction time, with most buildings raised in four years, from 1696 to 1700. Therefore, there's so much harmony in its architecture. The history of the Grand Place dates back much earlier, though. It was first established in the 11th century and evolved soon after to become the political and economic centre for the city. The most famous building in the square is the town hall, known as the Hôtel de Ville, built in 1402. It was constructed to upstage the Stadhuis in the rival city of Bruges. Inside are said to be several magnificent rooms. The most charming rooms are the Maximilian Chamber, hung with Brussels tapestries, the Council Chamber with an incredible ceiling and tapestries by Victor Janssen, the great banqueting hall and the Marriage Chamber, and a room called the Escalier d'Honneur, with murals illustrating the history of Brussels.'

'Bravo, bravo,' I clap for her, and she blushes as people turn to look. 'A little uh,' I tease, and we both burst into laughter. 'I shudder to think what a lot will be then.'

We take pictures of the palace with my digital camera. I place her gloved hand in the crook of my elbow, and we continue our tour. Glancing down at the map, I check the next site.

'It says here that we're close to the Manneken Pis.'

'Oh boy. Let's walk faster,' she exclaims.

She tries dragging me along faster, but I refuse to move more quickly than my current speed.

'Argh,' she grunts at me, which only increases my amusement.

We finally get to the site, and I see a black statue of a

little boy peeing.

'Oh-oh, I love reading about this statue,' Yasmine exclaims. 'Okay, listen. We're currently at the Rue de l'Etuve, where Brussels' best-known landmark, the Manneken Pis, is situated. A crowd of tourists usually besiege it.'

'That is correct,' I pitch in, stretching my hands around to signify the crowd of people milling around and taking pictures. We laugh at this before she continues.

'Although the statue has been traced back to at least 1388, nothing much is known about the origin of this figure of a little boy urinating. The statue is referred to popularly as "the oldest citizen of Brussels." Various legends have been associated with the Manneken. According to one, the fountain is a tribute to a courageous infant who averted a conflagration. Another legend is that it commemorates the son of a prominent man who couldn't hold back the pressing urge to pee while taking part in a procession.'

'I'm tempted to agree with the second legend,' I say.

'A lot of people say it's definitely the second one,' she concurs. 'The statue was made in 1619 by Jerôme Duquesnoy and has been stolen on several occasions, though always recovered. You should know that during major celebrations and festivals in Brussels, the statue is famed for being dressed in costume,' she finishes.

I'm tempted to clap again, but I resist the urge to clap

when I remember how embarrassed she was the last time.

'Are you hungry?' I ask as I take her hand and put it back in my elbow, and we resume walking.

'Yeah, I could do with something to eat, but let's see one more place first.'

I approve, and we head to the next place on the map, Saint-Michel Cathedral. The Cathedral looks so imposing, and I'm awe-struck. I have a feeling I'll be awe-struck many times on this trip. I take lots of pictures of the building before motioning to Yasmine.

'Stand over there so I can take a picture of you with the building as a backdrop.'

She stands there, and I take many snaps of her before doing the same for myself.

'Do you know much about here?' I ask.

'I know very little, so let's listen to that tour guide explain.' She points to a group of people close to us who are being led by a man we assume is the tour guide, as they all are raptly listening to him speak. We move closer to them and listen.

'Dedicated to St. Michael and St. Gudula, who are the patron saints of Brussels, this Gothic church was first founded in 1225 but was completed in the 15th century.' I turn to see the impressive facade, rising majestically above a broad flight of steps and crowned with twin towers. The tour guide is still speaking. 'Designed by Jan van Ruysbroeck, the beautifully proportioned interior is 108 meters by 50 meters and is lavishly furnished. It's home to some outstanding stained-glass windows created by Bernard van Orley. A transept depicting Charles V and Isabella of Portugal is located in the south, and the transept of the Hungarian royal pair Louis II and Mary is in the north. We also have there the Chapel of the Holy Sacrament. To the left of the choir, there's a window illustrating the story of the Miracle of the Host.'

The group moves away from us and goes elsewhere. I look beside me to see Yasmine taking pictures with my camera. She yawns unexpectedly, and I shake my head slowly.

'It's time to eat, princess,' I say as she grabs hold of my hands.

We move to the part of Brussels where there are a series of shops selling everything and anything. We locate a restaurant that looks promising and walk in to have our fill of food. Our bill comes with a box, and when we open it, we see chocolates inside. The manager of the restaurant comes up to us with a big smile.

'You can't come to Belgium and not eat any of our chocolates.'

'How do you know we're tourists?' Yasmine inquires.

'Well, the camera on your neck gives you away quite easily,' he replies with a raucous laugh.

We thank him profusely and tip generously before leaving the restaurant. There are a series of small shops in the street where the restaurant is located, so we decide to do a bit of window shopping.

'Let's get something from some of the local shops,' I suggest.

'Yes. I did promise Charlotte and Mum that I'd get them lots of knickknacks,' Yasmine replies, and we move closer to the shops to identify anyone that catches our fancy.

A few shops away from the restaurant, there's a little corner shop. What sets it apart from the other shops is that it looks so out of place on the colourful street. The shop is painted brown with equally brown doors and very few Christmas decorations. However, the items hanging from its window look interesting, and we move closer. There isn't a sign hanging anywhere, and we don't know what the shop sells. The door opens as we approach the shop, and a woman dressed in heavy clothing walks out. Her hair is brown and stringy, and she has a disgruntled face. Thick billowing coats cover her entirely from her neck to her feet. From where I stand, I can see that her hair needs washing.

'Please come on in, my dears,' she motions to us.

'Erm, we were just looking thro...' Yasmine attempts to explain, but the woman waves her off.

'You can browse through the shelves while you warm

up. Just come in out of the cold first,' she ushers us into the shop.

Yasmine grabs hold of my hand as we go inside after her, but we stay by the entrance. The shop looks even worse inside. Strange ornaments adorn the shelves, and candles are lit in various corners of the shop. The lit candles make no sense as the shop is well lit.

'So, what do you sell?' Yasmine asks the woman who is warming herself by the fireplace.

'I do readings of palms and a little of everything spiritual.'

'Reading of palms,' I quip, 'can you tell what's going to happen and what has already happened by reading someone's palms?'

'Yes, I can,' she boldly replies.

I turn to Yasmine, and we share an amused smile.

'Let us talk privately for a moment,' I say to the woman, and she retreats into a back room, giving us privacy.

'What do you think?' I ask, 'it sounds phoney, but it could be fun.'

'Yes, it's definitely phoney, but I don't want to do it.'

'Any particular reason?' I inquire.

'No,' her brows furrow as she contemplates something, 'she gives me the creeps.'

'Okay. Let's just look around her shop, then go.'

She nods her head at this, and we walk around the shop,

looking at the shelves and jars with unknown contents. It's at this moment that the lady walks back into the shop.

'So, have you decided?' She looks at us.

'Yeah, we have decided not to do the palm reading. We're not too comfortable with that,' I reply.

Yasmine gives me a relieved smile. I think she thought I would make her seem like a fearful woman.

'If you don't want the palm reading, it's okay,' the woman continues, 'I can just check your auras. It'll be fun.'

Yasmine and I turn to look at each other again. She shrugs her shoulder, so we both turn back to the woman and accept.

'Great, let's go into the next room where we'll have more privacy.'

She leads us to a room curtained off from the rest of the shop. When we step in, the smell of incense and candles bombard us. She certainly has a thing for candles. I think to myself. She motions for us to sit down, so we settle down on the floor, and watch as she lights candles around us in a circle. She brings some strange-looking dolls and places them away from the candles before bringing forward something unexpected. An enormous book is placed right in the middle of our half circle.

'Okay, pay attention,' she says as she sits down on the other side of the circle. 'All I want you to do is hold hands and stay silent until I tell you to talk. Laughing is allowed, but no side talk and no cutting me off.'

When we nod, she holds each of our hands and motions us to hold each other's hands, making it a circle. She looks at the book open before her and reads from it; the words make little sense to me. They sound eerily strange, but she quickly stops and looks at Yasmine.

'You have a lot of energy around you, not all of it good. You have a troubled aura, and creatures are moving all around it.'

I feel Yasmine's eyes move to me and fight to hold back the laughter bubbling in my throat. Remembering her rules, we keep quiet.

'The energy around you needs to go. Close your eyes,' she commands.

We do so because we have come too far to stand up now. When I see Yasmine close her eyes, I do the same. The woman's words change. I don't understand it, but I know that things feel different. I feel a chill on my skin, and struggle to keep my eyes closed until she tells us to open them. I turn to look at Yasmine and notice that she looks very pale.

'Jace, please let's go.'

She doesn't have to tell me twice. I uncurl my body from its seated position and guide her to her feet. I pay the woman her fee, and we move outside.

'Yasmine, what's wrong?'

'I started feeling dizzy when she was saying those strange words,' she replies. 'It must be tiredness.'

'Do you want to end Brussel's tour here so you can go rest?' I ask, feeling worried.

'No, of course not,' she laughs. 'Let's get out of here and go somewhere else.'

Yasmine Belmont

I feel strange. My head feels heavy, and my hands feel clammy. That woman was creepy, and her shop gave me such a bad feeling. We walk along the busy streets, looking at sights and marvelling at the beauty of Brussels. Jace looks down at his map before he lifts his eyes to me.

'The Royal Museum of Fine Arts of Belgium is just a few minutes' walk from here.'

My heart skips with excitement.

'Oh my God, oh my God, let's go.' I make a run for it, or at least attempt to. I can hear Jace's laughter as he pulls me back.

'Easy, princess. We'll get there without having to run.'

I laugh at my excitement. I guess I'm too pumped up. Jace grabs hold of my hands, and together, we walk hand in hand until we get to the museum. We buy tickets and are ushered inside. I love museums. The serenity, the centuries of work, and the things those paintings and portraits have seen make it very awe-inspiring.

'Oh, I love reading about this museum,' I exclaim.

Jace looks surprised beside me. 'You know some things about the museum?'

'Yes, I do. Care to hear it?'

'Please go ahead,' he lets go of my hands and motions for me to start.

'The Royal Museum of Fine Arts of Belgium is a group of art museums. They include six museums: the Old Masters Museum, the Magritte Museum, the Fin-de-siècle Museum, the Antoine Wiertz Museum, and the Constantin Meunier Museum. They contain over 20,000 sculptures and paintings, and the dates range from the 15th century to the 21st century. Napoleon Bonaparte founded it in 1801 but opened in 1803. It houses a great number of works from the Flemish school and several masterpieces by Pieter Bruegel, the Elder, who was a masterpiece artist,' I explain. He looks wowed that I know all this, but I can't reply to him because it's then that I catch sight of Pieter Bruegel, the elder's paintings. 'Jace, look. There are his paintings.'

I hurry forward, and I can hear him come up beside me. There's a range of magnificent paintings behind a roped-off area, and they transfix me. I only know about a few of them. After looking at them and taking a series of pictures, I move to another section. There's a little corridor behind this section. It seems to be where the guards are positioned, but now there's no guard, and the area looks kind of dark. Oh, wait, someone is standing there. I squint my eyes but can't make out if it's a guard or not. Even if it is a guard, why would he be standing so far back? This figure is facing the left wall, but it suddenly turns in my direction, and I can feel its gaze on me. What is he doing?

'Jace,' I call, and he walks closer to me, 'why is that security guard acting so strange?'

I turn to see Jace squinting his eyes before turning to look at me with a confused expression.

'I don't see anyone there, Yasmine. Who are you referring to?'

Surprised, I concentrate harder on the figure, and my eyes widen when I see he has something protruding from his stomach. My initial assessment had been that it's a shield or sword of some sort at its side, but it looks like something is coming out from its stomach itself. It seems like someone had put something through him, and I can't understand why Jace can't see him.

'He's standing right there, Jace. Look closer.'

Jace moves as close as he can and squints harder, but still turns to look at me with a baffled expression.

'Yasmine, there's no one there.' When he sees how my eyes widen in shock, he puts his hand on my back and gently guides me away from there. 'I think the enclosed space is playing with your head.'

'Yes, I think so too,' I agree. 'Why don't we go outside?'

We go outside the museum and head down the stairs. I feel so confused right now because I know what I saw. How is it that Jace couldn't see it as well? Am I hallucinating? Did I hit my head somewhere? Jace comes in front of me and halts my movement.

'Princess, let's forget about that, okay? You're probably tired, and it's getting late. Why don't we go on back to the hotel where you can relax?'

I smile at his sweetness and marvel silently at how he cares so much about me.

'It's getting late, and I'm tired, but before we end our Brussels tour, let's visit one more place,' I ask as I feel my good spirits returning.

He smiles at me, and the smile paired with his shining eyes makes me want to hug him, but I grab hold of his hand, and we walk silently towards the next place in mind, the Chateau Royale. When we approach the park, I feel relief flow through me. The lush green grass, beautiful, imposing structure, and peaceful atmosphere is very calming, well as calming as a park full of people can be. Jace has already begun taking pictures of everything and motions for me to pose for a photo. I smile and pose for different shots with the beautiful park surrounding me. I then take the camera from him and take pictures of him, but it doesn't take him long to refuse to pose for anymore.

'Well, Miss tourist guide, what do you know about here?' He inquires.

'Okay, here it goes.' I clear my throat. 'This place is known as the Chateau Royale. It's the home of the Belgian Royal Family, and although it's not open to the public, the park surrounding it at Laeken is. There are delightful footpaths and several attractions that interest tourists. We have the monument to Leopold I at the centre of the circular flowerbed in front of the palace. There's also the Japanese Tower, in the northern corner of the park, which was originally built for the Paris Exhibition of 1900 and has garnered quite a lot of tourist attention. The hothouses were erected in Leopold II's time and are the highlight of the gardens. They are open to the public during April and May when many of the plants have flowers in bloom, which sadly is not now, so we can't see the hothouses.'

He applauds my speech, and I do a little curtsy, making us laugh.

'I should be paying you for this,' he says as he shakes his head.

We see some benches placed for the public and pick one in an area with few people milling about. The shade above the bench is a blessing. We dust the snow off the chairs before sitting down and facing the park. Jace moves closer to me and wraps his arm around my shoulders, and I lean into the warmth he provides.

'How are you feeling now?' He asks, and I smile.

'I feel great. Thank you for agreeing to come to the park.' He leans closer, and I feel his lips touch my forehead in a way that feels comforting.

'Do you remember we said that we'll tell each other our deepest, darkest secrets at the places we go to?' he asks, and I instantly remember.

'Yes,' I reply and turn to look at him.

'Well, my secret is too dark, and I don't feel comfortable talking about it here.'

'Why don't we go back to the hotel room where we'll have privacy to talk?' I suggest, and he seems to agree with me because he stands up and pulls me up too.

'Let's go get a cab then,' he says as we head out of Brussels.

Heading back to the hotel is very easy. The cab stops us right in front of it, and we proceed to our room. Once we close the door to the room behind us, I feel relieved. Jace moves into the bathroom and comes out a short while later.

'I've checked the bathroom, and it has all the essentials. Why don't you go have a hot shower and relax from the cold?'

I take his advice and move into the bathroom for a hot shower. I choose to dress in there, and when I'm out, he goes in for his shower.

Jace Tanner

I come out to see Yasmine sitting on the bed with the camera in her hand and the box of chocolates lying on the side table.

'I'm just looking through our pictures,' she murmurs without raising her head from the camera's screen.

She's wearing grey sweatpants with a long-sleeved shirt bunched up in front, which puts her stomach in full view. Her skin looks so silky. I'm salivating already. She looks up and smiles at me before noticing the way I'm looking at her. I don't know what she's thinking, but it makes a blush rise to her cheeks.

'So,' she begins, 'what did you want to talk about?'

I sit down in front of her and lower my head in shame. My tongue feels weighed down with the weight of the words I want to say.

'You know you can trust me, Jace.' Her soft palms take

hold of mine.

I marvel at the contrast between my hard palms, callused by years of guitar playing and rough work, and her soft palms that feel as if she's seen no evil in life, although I know that to be a lie. Gathering courage, I exhale a breath before I start to speak.

'When Aiden died, and my drugs problem got worse, I did something idiotic.' I close my eyes tightly because I don't want to see her reaction to what I'm about to say. 'I got incredibly suicidal, Yasmine, and I contemplated killing myself because of the guilt I felt. One night, in particular, I tied a rope around a beam in my room but couldn't summon the courage to do it. So, I drank bottles of hard alcohol to give myself the courage to kill myself. What happened was that I got incredibly intoxicated, and when I stepped up to the rope, I, fortunately, lost consciousness.' I open my eyes to see Yasmine's shocked face with tears streaming down her face. I can't bear to look at her and quickly shut my eyes again. 'I awoke to find myself sleeping in my vomit with the rope tied on a beam above me. Regret coursed through me like water and the fear of what I'd almost done. Jesus, I've never cried like I cried that day.'

Yasmine bursts into tears and drags me close to her as she hugs me tight.

'Jace, you almost died,' she cries.

'Shhh, I'm alright now, princess. I'm alright.' I pat her hair gently as she cries while calming myself as well. After a while, she straightens up and gently wipes my tears using her hands. 'I'm alright,' I repeat.

'You're alright,' she responds, as if looking for confirmation.

I pull her back to me and hug her again. She turns her head to the side and releases a sigh.

'I have something no one knows, too.' I release her to straighten up, and she wipes her red eyes again. 'When my dad was recently separated from us, and we came to live in France with my grandmother, Maman, I tried running away to meet my dad. I know, I know, I was stupid, but I was a child and didn't understand why my dad would try to hurt Mummy, so I resolved it in my little heart to meet him and talk to him. Phone calls from him were not allowed at home, so I decided to run from Paris back to America.' We burst into laughter at this. 'Well, I had succeeded in going out the front door. Mum had gone out and wasn't back yet, and Maman was in her room resting. I had just managed to hide in the thick shrubs we had beside the house when my mum came back from another job search. I saw her come out of the car and sit on the front porch with her head in her hands. My grandmother came out of the house and sat down quietly with her. Maman knew she had been rejected at another job interview and just held out her hand for an embrace. My mum threw herself into her mother's hands and wept bitterly. I heard her tell Maman through her tears, "Mother, how am I going to survive with my child? Everything is so difficult. Starting over is so difficult." Maman told her something. She said, "When things seem difficult, always remember why you're doing it. You're doing it for your daughter. That girl believes in you and sees you as her everything, and that is why you're working so hard. So let her believe in you, fuel you up. You can survive, you can thrive, and you will do this. If not for anything, do it for your daughter." My mum wiped her tears and smiled at her mother. She stood up, dusted off her clothes, and said, "Tomorrow is another day to try again," and Maman smiled at her as they walked inside. I heard everything so clearly from my position in the shrubs and started crying. She had given up everything for me, and I was here trying to make it more difficult for her. I just stood up from my crouching position, dusted off my clothes, and walked inside the house. I've told no one about this, and I like to pretend that it never happened.' She finished with a sad smile, and I moved my head to hers and dropped a light, sweet kiss on her lips.

'You've always been a considerate person. That reminds me,' I continue, 'you said you wanted to ask me something when we were about to leave the hotel this morning.'

'Yes, that's right,' she perks up when she remembers,

'Forgive me. I know it's intrusive, but I thought when the band fell apart, you lost all your money on drugs and rehab. This trip is quite lavish, and we're staying in five-star hotels getting the VIP treatment. Where is the money coming from?'

I laugh out loud at this. 'Yasmine, the money did not finish. When a group has a highly successful album and lots of sold-out shows, money flows in unreservedly, especially when you have a management team as incredible as we did. When I started blowing money on drugs, I barely touched my money as I used money from television shows and other miscellaneous cash. The real money was locked away in a fixed deposit by my sister and me years ago. So, I'm not broke.' She joins in on the laughter with a sheepish expression.

'I'm sorry. I just wanted to make sure that you weren't spending your last money on this trip just to impress me.'

I assure her that it isn't like that, and we settle down to eat our chocolates.

'I have to call my mum,' she tells me.

'Yes, I'll call my sister while you call your mum.'

We finish up and then prepare for bed because we have a long day tomorrow. The Belgium tour was complete; day 1 of our tour is over. Tomorrow we leave for the Netherlands.

Stomping through the forest grounds, I feel sticks break under my feet. I can hardly breathe, but the breathing of the creature chasing after me is giving me excess doses of adrenaline. The forest is dark, and the only light is coming through spaces in the foliage. I use the little available light to guide my steps as I run. The creature gets closer and closer. Its breathing terrifies me, and I would do anything to escape it. I don't want to look, but I need to know how close it is to me. I turn my head and, in the process, I trip on a log of wood. Fear swallows me whole as I roll around on the ground. I quickly jump up and turn to face my fear. The sight before me makes my eyes widen. This is no creature. This is a man that a sharp piece of wood has impaled. The wood sticks out of his stomach while blood still drips down. His head is mangled beyond recognition, and the only thing that stands out in his face are his eyes, which look as wild as crazed dogs' eyes. His cloth looks tattered and bloody. The scariest part is that he's holding a sharp piece of wood in his hand and gazing at me. I take careful steps back, keeping my eye on him, but at that moment, he runs at full speed towards me, and I scream until everything goes black.

I jump up from the bed with sweat dripping down my

body, which is already in a state of flight. I look crazily around me to see Yasmine still sleeping soundly next to me.

'So, it was a dream?' I ask myself as my heartbeat returns to normal.

I vividly remember everything that happened in that dream, and it's strange because I rarely remember my dreams. This is the craziest dream I've ever had, and it feels all too real to me. I look at my phone on the bedside table and see that it's 2am. I don't think I'll be able to go back to sleep, so I turn towards Yasmine. She is sleeping facing away from me, so I pull her closer to me, breathe in the scent of her hair and embrace the comfort her warmth brings. I lay like that until morning.

In the morning, the hotel serves us breakfast comprising waffles, syrup, and an assortment of other meals that Yasmine seems to enjoy immensely. I thank the woman who delivered it and eat it mindlessly. I know Yasmine has noticed my contemplative disposition, and she asks me what's wrong, but I tell her not to worry.

After breakfast, we dress up, pick up our bags, and head out of the hotel. I settle the bills upfront, and we get into the taxi that's waiting to take us to the train station. We arrive at Brussels-Midi station and settle down in first-class. The train takes us to Amsterdam Central station where we'll get a taxi to take us to the hotel.

'So, where are we going to first?' Yasmine inquires

excitedly.

'I think we'll head for lunch first at one of the popular restaurants,' I reply. My mood has brightened up, and I'm now back to my usual self, but the dream is still on my mind.

'Let's go to The Grasshopper steakhouse. I've read so much about it,' she says.

'What do you know about it?' I ask.

'Well,' she starts, 'The Grasshopper steakhouse in Amsterdam is a rustic, wood-panelled steakhouse offering city views from a magnificent property. It overlooks the canals with boats tied to posts awaiting the next day's use in the evenings. It's a building with three floors. One floor houses a coffee shop, one houses a steakhouse, and the other houses a Grand Cafe. It's a trendy restaurant with excellent reviews.'

'That sounds fantastic,' I say.

She clears her throat before she speaks again. 'Why were you so restless this morning? Did something happen?'

'I had an upsetting dream early this morning, and I don't understand the dream enough to explain it.'

She places her hand on top of mine that I had splayed on the table.

'Just try to get your mind off it. In a few hours, you'll forget about it.'

I smile at her, and we sit there making small talk

until the train arrives at Amsterdam central. A cab takes us to the hotel, where we freshen up and get dressed. By now, it is noon, and we decide to eat at The Grasshopper steakhouse. Using a cab takes the shortest time from the hotel, and we're quickly directed to the floor where food is sold. There are a lot of people there, and the restaurant appears to be full. Food and drinks are served, and by the time we're done, we decide that it has certainly lived up to its reputation. Boats are returning from their travels, and the sight of all the boats leisurely moving is so calming that I wouldn't be surprised if people often fall asleep here. I turn to look at Yasmine, who seems equally entranced by the sight.

'So beautiful,' I say, looking at her.

'I know, right,' she replies, smiling.

She turns to see that I'm referring to her and smiles sweetly at me before leaning across the table to give me a kiss, which is too short for my liking.

'Let's pay so we can head to someplace else,' I murmur, but she hears me clearly and picks up her purse. We pay the bills and decide to stroll to the next spot.

'So, we didn't get an itinerary, but let's get one tomorrow. As for now, how about we visit the Royal Palace Amsterdam?' she says and turns to me for confirmation.

I'm just thinking about how soft her skin seems and wondering if it's that soft everywhere. I can feel my eyes darken at my thoughts, and I know that's what she sees, which makes her at a loss for words.

'Jace,' she calls, confusedly.

Holding her hand, I lead her towards a row of trees with snow-covered leaves.

'Jace, what's happening?'

'I need to kiss you. It embarrassed you when people watched us kiss back in Paris, so I want to give us some privacy.'

'You want to kiss me?' she repeats.

I grin at the fact that that's where her thoughts appear to be stuck. I push her against a tree. Her thick coat will protect her from the cold in the trees.

'Yes, I want to kiss you,' I say.

I bring my hand up to her face and push back a strand of hair that had escaped from her beanie. Her face is soft yet cold, and her lips look inviting. I just want to taste it, taste her. She brings her face closer to mine as we stare into each other's eyes. We meet in a soft, deep kiss. Our lips fit so well together, as if they were meant for each other. She releases a soft sigh when I part her lips and moves her body closer to mine. I suck gently on her bottom lip before sliding my tongue inside the warmth of her mouth. God, I missed her warmth. My hand goes to her waist and moves down to cup her ass through her trousers. Fuck, we need to stop. She makes a noise of protest deep in her throat when I pull away from her. Her lips look so soft, pink, and swollen, and looking at her makes me groan and step further away from her.

'One more minute of this, and I'll have you spread before me on any available surface,' I tell her when it seems she wants to protest.

A shocked expression replaces her previous expression. I'm not an exhibitionist, but I don't care what people think when it comes to her.

'Erm... okay... I, erm guess,' she stammers, and I motion towards where we'd walked in.

'After you. Let's head on to the Royal Palace Amsterdam.'

She proceeds, and I follow her from a distance. Within a short while, I move up to her side and take her hand. We walk to the Palace in that manner. When we get close enough to the Palace, I'm equally in awe. How were such impressive buildings made back then? This looks so powerful. I turn to Yasmine, who struggles to turn on the camera in her jacket. When she has accomplished that, she takes endless photos of the Palace.

'Let me take a picture of you,' she insists excitedly.

I oblige and pose for many takes before taking the camera from her and telling her it's her turn to pose for pictures. The Palace looks excellent as a background for her pictures, and when we're done taking photographs, she begins to tell me about the Palace.

'The Royal Palace Amsterdam is a reception palace for the ruler of Amsterdam, King Willem-Alexander. In addition, the Palace is open to visitors as much as possible so we can take a tour of it if we want. The Palace was constructed in the 17th century, making it the largest and most prestigious building from that century. It's one of The Netherlands' most important monuments. The Royal Palace is one of three palaces in the Netherlands which is located on the west side of Dam Square. Dam square is not too far from where we stand and is a town square right in the centre of Amsterdam. The Palace is also opposite the war memorial,' she points at a monument very close to the Palace. 'The war memorial is a monument designed by Jacobus Oud where the National remembrance of the Dead ceremony is held on every 4th of May to commemorate those who died in World War II and subsequent armed conflicts. The Palace is also situated next to the Nieuwe Kerk, a 15th-century church,' she completes. 'Actually,' she says again, 'don't think I know all these places at the drop of a hat. I brought some books with me that explain the tourist sites in each country, and I've been reading up on them.'

'That was great. It doesn't even matter that you have a book. The fact that you remember all those things is awe-inspiring. Now, do you want to see the palace?' I ask.

'Oh yes,' she literally jumps.

'I got tickets for the both of us. It's very affordable,' I say as we walk to the entrance.

'This is so amazing,' she gushes. 'I hope pictures are allowed.'

'We'll have to find out.'

Chapter Five

We walk to the palace entrance, where we're directed inside by an older woman. Going in, we meet a crowd of people, and I'm thankful that we came at such a time. As it's winter, groups of visitors have dramatically reduced compared to the crowd that would have been here in summer or spring.

'Your tickets please,' a man just after the entrance asks. We show him our tickets, and he points us towards a group of about seven people. 'You're joining them for the tour. A guide will be around shortly,' the man instructs, and we walk to join the group.

In a few minutes, a short and balding man comes to stand in front of us.

'Hello everyone,' he begins, 'I'm Mr Albert, and I'll be your tour guide. Please let's begin.' We trail after him as he leads the group. 'There are twenty-one stops during this tour, and it's estimated to last for an hour, so buckle up.'

Albert informs us that only the first floor is available for visiting, and I see Yasmine's face fall at this information. It seems she really wanted to see everything.

Yasmine Belmont

Our guide tells us that only the first floor is available for touring, and my expression falls. Oh well, it's better than nothing. The palace's interior is of such a royal class, and the atmosphere is so warm that I feel like a reigning royalty myself. There are a lot of stops and a lot of tiny rooms where the tour guide explains their history. It turns out that officials use a lot of these rooms for meetings. It makes me wonder what these walls have heard, and all the history enclosed in them.

'Agencies are developing technology to enhance these palace tours,' the tour guide continues, 'in a couple of years, there will be no human tour guide for the palace anymore. Instead, there will be audio tours where you get to listen to everything extensively.'

Wow, that's incredible. Technology is advancing rapidly. Many people in the crowd have the same reaction of awe as I do. There are a lot of corners and short corridors that lead to nowhere in the palace, and we walk right past them. A hand touches mine, and my eyes trace it to see that Jace is touching me. I meet his eyes, which are dancing with happiness, and my lips automatically smile back.

'Are you enjoying the tour so far?' I ask.

'Yes,' he replies, 'it promises to be very enjoyable.'

We trail after the tour guide, who continues leading

us from one stop to another, all the while explaining the history of each spot. The tour group moves past a corridor to the next stop, which is historically similar to the other rooms. As I follow them, I catch sight of someone walking down the corridor. Oh no, the person probably doesn't know that the hallway doesn't lead anywhere. I move back from Jace's side, and he looks back curiously. When he sees that I'm okay, he resumes his original position and starts taking pictures of the sights in the palace. I move into the corridor, which is a bit deeper than the other corridors I've seen. The figure is still moving, and because the corridor is poorly lit, I can't make out more than a silhouette of what looks like a man.

'Excuse me, sir. This corridor doesn't lead anywhere,' I call out, but he doesn't acknowledge me.

He rounds a corner, and I debate going back outside.

'No, I've come too far to go back now.'

I decide to find out where he's headed, and I follow him. To my shock, the corner he rounds off at is precisely where the corridor stops, but no one is there. I feel goosebumps as it dawns on me that the figure has disappeared with no explanation. Maybe I've been seeing things that don't exist.

'Okay.' I begin to retreat, 'it's high time I left this corridor. It's obvious that closed off palaces and other closed off sites are not my cup of tea. I must be seeing things again.' Taking slow, measured steps, I back away slowly, feeling hesitant to turn my back to the wall. 'I'm just being paranoid for no reason at all,' I mutter under my breath.

I don't know if I imagine this too, but the air around suddenly gets colder. I'm wearing layers of clothing because of the season; this cold seems to permeate through my clothes, straight into my bones. I walk backwards slowly, moving my eyes frantically and hoping that no one sees me acting so weird. Once I round the corner and the path out of the corridor is straight, I breathe out a sigh of relief. 'Thank God, I can see everyone from here. Jace must be worried by now.'

I finally turn to face the entrance and increase my steps to get out of there as fast as possible. In my haste to rush out, my feet collide with something hard.

'Ouch,' I exclaim, 'Goddammit, that hurt.'

Now, wait a second. When I was coming into the corridor, I remember vividly that the path inside was empty, and nothing should have been there. I glance down to find out if I'm right or not. Nothing is blocking the corridor. What did I hit my feet on then? It's at that moment that I feel a presence behind me.

'Oh Lord, I'm going out of my mind in this place.'

I resume my walk out of the corridor, but the feeling that there's someone behind me gets stronger and stronger.

A tiny look back won't hurt, I think, and decide to crank my neck just a little to the back to reassure myself. With my feet moving towards the corridor entrance, I turn my head to the right and look over my shoulder. My eyes bulge out, and a terrifying scream rips out of my lungs at the ghastly sight behind me. I have never seen anything like this. What looks like a man, with soulless eyes and the pallor of a dead person, is staring back at me. His clothes can't even be called clothes, they are rags, and his head is shaved clean, giving a clear view of the progressive physical decay. His head is half-rotten, and his mouth drips blood. Apart from the fact that I'm staring at a dead person, what scares me the most is that he has a wooden stake protruding from his stomach. A hand grabs ahold of me from behind, and that's when I realise that I'm still screaming.

'Yasmine, what's wrong?' I turn to face a concerned Jace staring at me in panic. The tears stream from my eyes.

'Jace, let's run. It's trying to kill me. Please let's go,' I ignore his question and grab his arms to pull him along with me, but he stands his ground and grabs me in a tight hug. I don't understand why he's hugging me here. Isn't he scared of this creature?

'Who's after you, young lady?' A voice from my right says, and I turn to face the speaker. Our tour guide stares at me, half concerned, half wary. There's a crowd of people standing around me.

'Wait,' I wipe my tears, strengthened by the fact that Jace is standing right next to me, 'you mean that you all can't see him?'

The tour guide's face is wiped entirely clean of concern and now looks full-on wary.

'Yasmine, baby, there's no one here,' Jace replies, and I turn slowly to look at him. His brows furrow, and confusion shines in his eyes. I turn to where that monstrosity stood, and there's nothing but space.

'Do we need to call an ambulance?' a young woman asks. 'Maybe you hit your head on something and have a concussion?'

My face turns hot with shame, but my heart is still galloping wildly from the sight I'm very sure I saw.

'Yes, I did hit my head, but I'll go to the hospital by myself.'

Jace looks at me worriedly, then nods, 'yes, I'll take her to the hospital right away.'

'Okay, son. If you're sure,' the tour guide responds before they all move out of the corridor.

Some people look at me like I'm sick. I don't want to stay in this place for one more second and tell Jace just as much. He takes my hand and hurriedly leads me out of the corridor. We make our way out of the palace, and it seems to me as if everyone is parting the way for us. Eyes follow us, and fingers are pointing at me. I reflexively curl my body into Jace's side, and he puts a hand over my shoulder. A sigh of relief escapes from my lips as we descend the stairs. I grip on tightly to Jace's hand, still too shocked to speak. My mind is buzzing with thoughts. How is it that no one saw that thing? It's the second time I've seen something of the sort. Although it wasn't clear the first time, the figure is exactly like the one I saw today, and I know what I saw. No one can convince me that I didn't see it. Am I going crazy? Was there something in my food that's making me hallucinate? What is going on here? I'm shaken out of my thoughts when Jace detangles his hand from mine and turns me to face him. I was too preoccupied to notice that we had walked a short distance away from the Royal Palace. We're now standing under a shed.

'Yasmine,' he says, but I cut him off.

'Jace, listen, I know what I saw.'

'I'm not doubting you. I believe you, but I don't want you to speak about it now. You are shaking, and it's not from the cold.'

At his words, I come to realise that my body is trembling slightly from the fear of what I saw.

'Let's call it a day and head back to the hotel room. I want you warm and rested before we speak about what happened today.'

I nod numbly before exhaling deeply.

'You're right. I can't focus on anything now. Let's go

back to the hotel.'

We head back to the hotel, which is in central Amsterdam. Jace leads the way up the stairs and opens the door to let us into the room. I walk straight to the bathroom and strip before getting into the shower. Once I'm out, I see that Jace has ordered hot cups of tea or coffee; I'm not sure.

'These are relaxing teas. Apparently, the hotel restaurant serves them too,' he explains.

I sit on the bed and cross my legs before bringing a cup to my lips. The cold seeps out of me as the drink slides down my throat. I end up downing two cups of tea, leaving only one for Jace.

'Sorry, I finished everything,' I say, feeling like a glutton.

He laughs. 'I got it all for you, anyway.'

He finishes his cup, then comes to sit behind me.

'Lean back on me and relax,' he instructs, and I gladly do as he says.

I feel so relaxed. Although what happened earlier is still prominent in my mind, it doesn't feel as terrible as it did then. His hand extends over my stomach and draws me closer to him as my head rests on his shoulder.

'If you feel better, I would like to know what happened at the Royal Palace.'

I'm so scared that he won't believe me, but the least I can do is try. I relate all that happened to him, not leaving out a single detail. When I finish up, the shivers resume at full force.

'Shh, it's okay,' he pulls me closer. 'I've got you.'

'Do you believe me, though?' I muster up the courage to ask.

'Yes, I believe you, but I think someone played a cruel trick on you.'

That makes sense. It honestly does because the only other viable option would make me appear utterly crazy.

'Do you want to end the tour?' he quietly suggests, and I don't think I've ever moved so fast. I quickly turn in his hands to face him.

'What? No way. Why would you even suggest that?'

'Easy tiger,' he lifts his hands to soothe me, 'it was just a suggestion.'

I turn back to resume my relaxed position and stay that way until my phone rings. I pick it up to see Mum's caller ID.

'I'll talk to my sister really quickly while you speak to your mum,' Jace says, as he extricates himself from me and moves to the opposite side of the room.

'Hello, Mum.'

'Hi honey,' comes her chirpy voice.

'Why are you sounding so prep?' I tease.

'Oh nothing, I'm just having a swell time. The resort is magical, and I'm so glad I came,' Mum replies.

'That's great to hear, Mum.'

'How are you and Jace doing?' she questions.

'We're doing great. We've visited so many places already.' I list out the places we've been to. The conversation extends for a more extended period before I end the call and decide to call Charlotte next.

'Hello, Queen of Europe,' she says as she picks up the call.

'Queen of Europe? Is that a thing?' I laugh.

'Well, you're going around Europe, and you already know so much about so many things, so the title is befitting,' she counters.

I missed her laugh and jest. Jace comes up behind me, and I turn to give him the phone.

'Here, speak to Charlotte.'

'Hello, Charlotte,' he says as he grabs my waist and pulls me closer.

'Hi, Jace,' she replies, and they continue their conversation.

My mind, however, is on Jace's hand that's moving over my waist, to my lower back, and then back to my waistline.

Once the conversation ends, he drops the call, faces me fully, and places a hot, slow kiss on my lips. I part my lips in acceptance, and my hand goes to his shoulder, where I hold on as he ravages my lips, parting, tasting, teasing, and licking. When we both pull away, we're struggling to catch our breaths. I stare up at him and see him looking at me with wonder in his eyes. I move to kiss him more, but a loud yawn escapes my lips at that very instant. Mortified, I place my palm over my mouth, but he only laughs at my reaction.

'Why are you blushing? You're just yawning because you're tired. Get on the bed so I can pull the covers over you.'

'I'm sorry we couldn't talk after the royal palace, but if you want, you can tell me about your secret,' I say, and he shakes his head.

'No, princess. You need to rest and not talk about anything sad,' he objects.

'Well, maybe I'm too strung up to talk, but listening to you talk will be helpful for me.'

'Okay,' he runs his hand through his hair, 'settle down and listen.'

I sit up and can see him debating with himself, but he seems to conclude that it would be therapeutic for him to tell someone about it.

'My father wasn't exactly a model husband,' he begins. 'He was a great dad and looked like an amazing dad, but I caught him cheating on my mum frequently. I remember coming into my parents' room to tell them about how my presentation in school had gone and seeing my dad and a random woman, both unclothed, on the bed. My father made me promise I wouldn't tell my mother, who had apparently gone out that morning. When I was seven years of age, I feared what he would do, so I kept it a secret. That was the first of several times I caught him. I felt too guilty to tell my mum as I had already kept it from her for a long time.'

'What he made you do was horrible,' I exclaim in shock, and I move to hug him.

'Yes, it was,' he replies. 'Nobody knows about it. Nobody. I'm too ashamed to tell Pearl.'

I hug him and lay his head on my shoulder. He then physically shakes off the thought and chuckles as he turns off the light, climbs into bed, and pulls the covers over us. Day two is over.

Jace comments, 'If we get a chance to come on another tour of Europe, let's not do it during this time,' and I agree wholeheartedly.

The weather is horrible and has been all morning. It's not even a drizzling kind of rain, but the heavy type that makes you want to curl up on a couch with a mug of hot chocolate and thick socks. Wait, did I hear him correctly? He said, "if we." Those words mean that he includes me in his future plans and would go on another tour with me. If so, then that makes me feel good in a way I can't explain. Checking my wristwatch, I groan at the time.

'It's almost noon, and we have spent the entire morning cooped up in the hotel.'

'Our appointment for our next stop is in thirty minutes,' Jace says despondently.

'Is it in a warm place?' I inquire since it seems like he's keeping one stop a secret from me.

'Yes, it is a warm place,' he replies.

A ray of sunlight pierces through the windows, and we look outside to see that the rain has now reduced to a light shower and the sun is fighting for dominance.

'The rain is stopping. Quick, let's get dressed.' I jump up from my spot in the hotel dining room and rush upstairs with Jace right behind me.

We get dressed and hurry out of the hotel. By now, thankfully, the rain has slowed to a drizzle, and we can comfortably walk under it.

'What's our first stop today?' I ask.

'We're first heading to the Heineken Experience, which is a short way from here according to this.' He looks down at the itinerary in his hand.

'The Heineken Experience? What's that?' He turns to look at me, surprise registered on his face.

'You don't know the Heineken Experience?' He asks,

looking amused.

'Well, don't be so surprised. I didn't say I know everywhere,' I reply with a laugh.

Jace takes hold of my hand and pulls me to his side. I've noticed that he loves doing this.

'The Heineken Experience is the first Heineken brewery, and it's in Amsterdam. That's all I know of it, but a tour has been arranged, so we'll get to learn more,' he explains.

'That sounds really nice,' I comment, but my eyes are darting everywhere, and unknown to me, he notices.

'What are you searching for?'

He makes me freeze. I think he sees my guilty expression and immediately understands what is going on. He brings one of my hands to his lips and lays a kiss on it.

'I've told you to calm down. I'm here with you. Soon we'll sort this out.'

I calm myself and hold tight to him until we get to a building with "The Heineken Experience" written on it.

'This is it,' he announces.

We walk into the building, and once we introduce ourselves and show some ID, the ma'tre d' ushers us in. A man comes to meet us and tells us he will be our guide.

'Hello, I'm Alec, a Heineken connoisseur and your private guide for this tour,' he announces before getting started. We stroll through the building as he speaks. 'A man named Gerard Adriaan Heineken founded Heineken in 1864. However, in 1988, the brewery was closed because of its inability to meet high demands. It opened again a few years later and has gone on to become the second-largest brewery in the world. This tour is expected to last for two and a half hours. It will include a tour of the historical brewery and exclusive access to a hidden bar,' he explains as we go behind the scenes to check out the brewery.

I keep looking at hidden corners and dark spaces around me, praying I don't see that creature again. Once the tour ends, we thank the guide and make our way outside. The sky has turned an ugly shade of grey, and it looks like rain is about to start again.

'We have one more stop today,' Jace startles me from my assessment of the sky.

'Where is that?' I ask curiously, but he only smirks at me.

'Don't worry about that, princess. When we get there, you'll see it,' he replies.

I'm this close to stamping my feet on the ground in annoyance.

'Come on, Jace. You've been keeping it secret since yesterday.'

'Patience, woman,' he laughs. 'You'll find out soon.'

I'm thankful we brought an umbrella with us because the rain resumes with no preamble. It quickly changes from a drizzle to a full-blown shower. We use our umbrella until we can call a taxi. Jace gives him the directions written on paper, and the cab drives until it stops at a white building with the name "RUSH" inscribed on the entrance.

I keep quiet until we walk to the entrance. Jace gives the doorman our appointment name and time, who ushers us in.

Jace finally explains, 'Well, Yasmine, I figured we both could do with a little massage, so I booked an appointment at what is promised to be a wonderful facility.'

I'm so excited, and I thank him profusely. We're shown our room, which has two beds for both of us. Our masseurs introduce themselves, and we change into towels and lie down for it to begin. The massage takes less than an hour; by the time we're done, I feel pampered, spoilt, and like all my tension has been squeezed out of me. We get dressed and thank them before heading out.

'Let's go get dinner,' Jace suggests. His face looks relaxed, the way I feel mine does. I have a different idea, though.

'Let's go back to the hotel and eat dinner at the restaurant?'

The afternoon is almost over, and we have no other stops for the day, so he agrees, and we get a taxi to drop us off. We stop by the hotel restaurant and have some food and a few drinks because we already had a complimentary glass of Heineken at the Heineken Experience. Jace wants to sit at the restaurant and enjoy watch the rain through the window, but I have other plans.

'Why don't we go upstairs?' I suggest.

He looks confused for a good minute before he shrugs. 'Okay. Let's go then.'

I lead the way upstairs, let myself into the room first, and take off my coat. He comes in next and looks at me questioningly before taking off his coat.

'I know it's not dark yet, and you're probably wondering why I said we should come in.' I start, and he gives me a little smile that says, "obviously." I stand up and move slowly towards where he's standing. 'How about I show you instead of telling you?' I say as I run a finger over his chest before standing on my toes to kiss him slowly. He pulls back and stares at me intensely. His eyes are full of questions, and I decide to answer what I think he wants to know. 'I know this seems direct, but we've been together for some time now. I mean, erm not together, together like y-you know dating but more like…' I stutter, but my speech trails off as his hands come to rest on my cheek.

'You don't have to be disturbed about our relationship, Princess. I know I'm kind of stupid for not asking you out formally. I don't want to do it now, so you won't think that you had to ask me to do it. Know that you are my woman, and I think I've loved you since the first night at your place.'

I feel my face get warm, but this time, it isn't a blush of embarrassment; but instead, one of pleasure. I lean up and kiss him gently, but he pulls back again.

'Are you sure about this? You are not doing it for any other reason than the fact that you want it, right? Your feelings matter to me.'

'I want it. I want you,' I murmur, mesmerised by his eyes, so brown and full of emotions.

With my reassurance, he leans down and finally kisses me. My lips surrender under his as he takes charge and uses his hand to tilt my jaw the way he wants. He licks at the seam of my lips, and I open for him. His tongue slides in and explores the crevices of my mouth, making my knees weak. His hand at my throat moves down to the small of my back and pulls me snugly against him. Every part of him is pressing against me, and I marvel at the strength in his body that clothes can't conceal. My tongue meets his, and a moan slips from my throat. When we're both breathless, we pull away and stare at each other, brown orbs to blue orbs. He bends down, and his hand at my back moves to the back of my knees. He carries me to the bed and sits me on it before easing back. I start to take off my top, but he beats me to it. Next are my shoes and pants. Once I'm in my bra and panties, he pulls back to stare at me. The raw hunger in his eyes has me feeling so restless. His face gets tighter, and he grunts before taking off his shirt. I scoot forward to help him, and we get his shirt, boots, and trousers off. In his briefs, he climbs on the bed and resumes our kiss. One hand caresses my face while the other reaches to unhook my bra. He grunts and moves away as my bra comes undone.

'You're so beautiful,' he whispers, taking a nipple in his mouth.

His hand caresses my other breast, rolling a nipple between his thumb and index finger. I gasp as the effect of his actions hits me. He brings his mouth back to mine. This time, there's nothing gentle about our kiss. It's all passion and wet kisses and curious hands. Jace's body pushes mine down, and he covers my body with kisses, moving to places I didn't expect, but I can't say I object. His passion reflects marvellously in his kisses and his hands during his pursuit of my pleasure. My moans get higher and higher, and I grab his head and drag him back up my body to kiss him. I taste my pleasure on his lips, which makes my blood hot. My hands creep into his hair, and I push through the softness of it. He pulls back to pull on a condom, and when he slides in me, our collective groans fill the room. It feels better than I ever imagined, this merging of our souls. Even while seeking his pleasure, he keeps mine at the forefront of his mind, kissing me as he moves in me. His thrusts coupled with the feeling of his body on me have me feeling sky high and in search of a release from this beautiful, beautiful pain. The movement of our bodies is so in sync; when he pulls back, I push forward. It's almost as if we're two parts of a machine, built to work together. He increases his thrusts, and the relief I'm searching for seems to be within my grasp. My hand tightens in his hair, and my other hand clings to the sheets as he beautifully ravages my body. His grunts spur me on faster. Suddenly I shoot over this evasive cliff and am catapulted into a space of blissful release that makes me lose the sense of my surroundings and makes my brain feel light. I come back to consciousness to hear my lips moving, and it's almost as if I was reciting a mantra.

'Jace, Jace, oh my God Jace, oh my God.'

He buries his face in my neck, and our laboured breathing fills the room. He places a sweet kiss on my forehead, and his lips stretch into a gleeful smile. He rolls off me and pulls my face to his to kiss me. I bury my face in his neck and breathe in his scent. I'm so addicted to the smell of him. His hand drags my body to his, and I snuggle up next to him.

'That was so incredible. You were amazing,' he comments with a big shit-eating grin.

'Well, you were pretty damn incredible also,' I reply and feel the damned blush coming back. He smiles mischievously

'I've always wondered if you blush only on your cheeks or if it extends to other places. I've realised that it does extend. You blush everywhere.'

I scream and burrow my head into his chest, 'stop teasing me.'

He laughs and pulls my face up for a kiss. I sigh into his mouth. He deepens the kiss, sucking on my lower lip, and runs his hand on my bare back. We pull away, and he stretches his hand over my waist. This position is so comfortable, and I'm so tired that I slip right into sleep.

I'm woken up when I try to switch my position but restricted by a body which I seem to be pressing against. Fighting to regain my consciousness, I open my eyes to see that my face is on Jace's chest, his naked chest, and recollections of what happened earlier flood me.

'Oh my, we actually did do it,' I say to myself, a slight smile playing on my lips.

And it was quite a delicious experience. Jace looks so peaceful in his sleep. His hard exterior and all the troubles in his life seem to have faded away, and he's left looking like a child with no worries. I go to the bathroom, get dressed in his shirt, and sit down on the couch. He wakes shortly after, and we order food and drinks to be brought up for dinner. After eating, we brush our teeth and go back to bed. According to Jace, tomorrow we head for Germany. Day 3 was beautiful and memorable.

The cab we take the following day drops us off at the entrance to Amsterdam Central Station. Jace speaks up, 'This is another place we're visiting, but we'll kill two birds with one stone. We have two hours before our train ride, so we'll use about an hour to explore.'

'That sounds great. I know a little about the station, though,' I say, to his amusement.

'A little from you is a lot.' Laughing, we walk to the entrance, taking in the imposing structure that is Amsterdam Central Station.

'Amsterdam Central Station in Amsterdam is the Netherlands' biggest public transport transfer spot and serves Amsterdam's visitors and inhabitants. It's the second busiest railway station in the country, serving approximately 250,000 people per day. It has 11 platforms and 15 tracks and was designed by the architect Pierre Cuypers, built by the contractor Philip Holzman and opened on 15 October 1889,' I explain, amused by his expression of shock.

'How do you remember all of this stuff?' he questions with a shocked expression.

At my laughter, he shakes his head and pulls me closer to himself. I've noticed that after yesterday's events, he's been acting extra close. He looks at me with an expression that makes me blush, which makes me remember what he said yesterday about my blush, making me blush more.

'Let's take a walk around and look at some sights,' he links his palm with mine, and we stroll around the station, dragging our bags behind us.

A few metres away from where we're standing, there's a spot that, strangely enough, is deserted. I find it odd because there's a sizeable crowd of people milling around in every direction, but this particular spot is quiet, very quiet. An eerie breeze flows past me, and the hair on my arms stand on end. I turn to Jace to ask if he feels strange and realise that he is staring right at the same place.

'Why is it so quiet all of a sudden?' he asks, and I notice that everywhere really has gone quiet.

Looking around us, people are still milling about and making a lot of noise, but it seems to us as if we have tucked all the noise into the background. We turn to look at each other with matching expressions of confusion and slight fear. A bulb lights up the spot out of nowhere.

'I didn't even know there was another bulb there,' I comment as Jace pulls me closer and puts his arm around my shoulder.

The spot is exceptionally bright now, and suddenly, all

the bulbs flicker off. The area is cloaked in darkness, and we wait with bated breaths. For what? We don't know, but it seems we both know that something is going on there. Squinting my eyes, I make out what seems like an outline of a person, and my heart jumps to my throat.

'Jace, I think there's…'

At that moment, bulbs flicker, and the object of my fear for many days now is standing right there. The way Jace freezes beside me indicates that this time, he has seen it, too.

'Yasmine, don't shout. It's just standing there. Let's retreat slowly, then maybe it won't notice until we get away,' Jace instructs in a terrified whisper.

I try to obey Jace's instruction and discreetly move my feet back. It looks terrifying in the full glare of light. It seems nothing less than a creature that has been dead for a very long time. Its head is half-rotten with giant fat maggots swimming in it. Its eyes look dead, emotionless and dark, and maggots are going in and coming out of them. Blood is pouring out steadily from the side of the mouth, and its skin looks ashen and dry. Its clothes could better be called rags, as there's little left in the top. The trousers, though, remind me of 15th-century clothing, and it's barefoot. The most prominent part of this monster is the stake embedded in its stomach. Is this how he died? Why is he here? What's going on? Jace's grip on my shoulder is so tight it would hurt if I paid attention to it. Our attention, however, is on this thing standing in front of us, staring quietly with its creepy eyes. We move our feet back one at a time, trying not to get noticed by it. When we've moved a few steps back, its head that was staring straight at us moves immediately to our feet before staring back at us. An audible gasp escapes my mouth. It noticed! As quick as a flash, it shakes its body and places one foot forward. Jace squeezes my hand. It's now or never. At a superhuman speed, it rushes towards us with an ugly snarl. I scream at the top of my lungs as Jace holds my hand, and we sprint away without looking back. We run faster than we've ever run and don't stop until we're out of the station. By now, tears are rapidly streaming down my face, and I don't want to stop running. Jace pulls me to a stop at a street lined with eateries and coffee houses. We dart our eyes everywhere, and I fear anyone approaching us or walking too close to us. When we're sure it's not anywhere near us, Jace pulls me in for a hug, and I cry into his coat. Passers-by don't disturb us, and we stay that way for a long while.

'Come on. Let's have a seat here,' he directs me to a seat at the nearest outdoor coffee shop. We sit in a spot that can only be accessed by one entrance and hold hands. 'Is that the same thing you saw in the Royal Palace?' He asks, and I nod. I'm overcome with fear and tears.

'You saw it also, right?' I ask to confirm because I don't know what I would do if I were the only person to see it.

'Yes, I did. I saw everything,' Jace replies.

'Thank you for believing me,' I squeeze his hands 'it was all I needed to feel better.'

'I must confess,' he begins, 'the reason I believed you so quickly is that I saw something exactly like that in my dream.' I'm shocked, to say the least. 'Do you remember that day I was very moody throughout the morning and wouldn't tell you the reason?' He asks, and I nod. 'That is the dream I had, and it left me feeling very disturbed.'

We sit there for a while. The time for our train ride has passed, but we're too terrified to go inside the station again. Later, we summon the courage and go inside to switch tickets and get another train to take us to Germany. We board the Dutch railway train and sit in our first-class seats. The ride starts, and we make several stops before crossing into Germany. After about three hours, the train arrives in Düsseldorf Hauptbahnhof.

'We're supposed to visit here for a tour,' Jace announces, and we look at each other contemplatively.

'Let's just go to the hotel. Tomorrow we'll come back to start the tour,' I suggest, and he agrees with me.

We leave the train station and get a cab to drive us to our hotel, where we're shown to our rooms. Before going in, we open the door and check the room from outside.

Once we're assured it's clear, we go in and freshen up.

'It's so ironic that this is happening,' Jace says.

'What do you mean?'

'Let me put it this way,' he continues, 'the dark secret I have to tell you today is quite horrible.'

I sit down on the couch and look at him carefully.

'When I was six, my mum told me that there was another sibling of mine. One I didn't know. She said he died before I was born. This made me so sad that I couldn't stop feeling down for days. So, one day in school, I heard that a new shop had opened in town. It's said that it was a soothsayer's shop, and that she did what we called "creepy things." An idea bloomed in my mind, and the next day, I snuck out of the house and went to the woman's shop. She thought I was a little kid playing pranks on her, but I later convinced her that I was serious. I told her I wanted to communicate with my brother and asked her if she could do it. She said yes, she could. She gave me instructions to sit down on a white line she drew with chalk, sprinkled something on me, and recited some strange words written in her book. I don't remember what happened next, but I think I fainted because I woke up to see myself lying down on the ground, and she was nowhere to be found. I ran out of there so fast and couldn't summon the courage to tell anyone.'

I'm so shocked at his story, but I grab hold of his hand

and squeeze it.

'My secret,' I begin, 'is that I had a classmate in middle school who proclaimed to be able to see ghosts. This should have made her creepy, but we were extraordinary children.' We laugh at this. 'It actually made her popular, and I wanted to be as popular as she was, so I asked her to help me see ghosts too. I went to her house for a sleepover, and she brought a little book out from the depths of her drawer. Then she told me to lie down, close my eyes and repeat after her. The words were bizarre, and I wondered how a little girl could know all this. I started getting creeped out and refused to continue with what I assumed was just a joke. She told me we needed to continue or there'd be dire consequences. I stood my ground and refused to continue. She just shook her head and refused to speak to me until the next morning. I remember fearing my own shadow for months after that.'

Although our stories are creepy, it seems to warm us up, and we prepare to go straight to bed. Moving closer to Jace, he pulls me impossibly closer with my back to his chest and pulls the cover over us before we go to sleep. Day four is finally over.

Jace Tanner

As Yasmine comes out to face me; all dressed and looking regal, I trail off, 'First stop today will be in...'

'You were saying?' she asks with raised brows.

'That you look impossibly beautiful,' I reply, and she laughs. I love making her laugh. She deserves it after the harrowing experience we had yesterday.

'Thank you, but really, where's our first stop?'

'It's at Aachen and...'

'Yesssssssss Aachen,' she screams and jumps to hug me.

'Why are you so happy about it being Aachen?' I question, although I'm happy that this place excites her.

'Erm, it's only the favourite place of Charlemagne.'

'Yes, that's true. I had forgotten that it's said he loved the hot springs, and his remains are said to be there,' I reply.

'Oooh,' she looks impressed and surprised all at once, 'someone knows their history.'

'Well,' I straighten my shirt and assume her stance, 'I know just a little about it.' This little act makes her laugh so hard that it's infectious, and before I know it, I'm also laughing.

We get dressed and go out of the hotel, get a cab, and settle in for the ride that is estimated to take over forty minutes. When we reach Aachen, the driver drops us off and we begin our exploration.

'Our private tour guide is meeting us in a few minutes,' I announce before noticing that she looks wary of everyone that's around us. I grab hold of her shoulder and turn her to face me. 'Listen, princess, we're safe. That incident happened in the Netherlands, and I don't think it will be here in Germany, okay?'

I see relief flood her eyes as she nods.

'Yes. I've heard you,' she says before breathing in and out deeply.

She takes my hand and directs us to a shaded area. A slim, middle-aged man introduces himself as Mr Collins, our tour guide.

'Let's begin,' he instructs, and we trail after him as he moves. 'Aachen, a spa city near Germany's borders with Belgium and the Netherlands, was a stronghold much favoured by Charlemagne. It's littered with hot springs, which the people of old believed to have healing properties. In the time of AD 936 to 1531, Aachen was the place of coronation for around thirty German kings.' He rounds off a corner while Yasmine and I listen carefully to him while staring at the sights. He stops in front of a mighty-looking building, which we're told is the Aachen Cathedral. The man continues, 'Aachen Cathedral, also called Imperial Cathedral, was one of Europe's first UNESCO world heritage sites and is one of the oldest buildings. Its Domschatzkammer, or treasury, has medieval artefacts, like the shrine of Charlemagne buried there in 814 AD. Charlemagne's marble throne and a golden reliquary contain his remains. It's also the resting place of Charlemagne.'

'He's very knowledgeable,' Yasmine whispers in my ear. I nod in agreement.

The guide leads us to what he describes as Aachen town hall. 'This hall is built on the remains of Charlemagne's original palace. It's the site of the magnificent coronation hall. On display are replicas of the imperial crown jewels and a portrait example, the portrait of Napoleon.'

This city is intensely regal looking, and the buildings add to its look. Yasmine looks around with wondrous eyes as the tour guide is explaining. I can understand what she's feeling. There's a lot of power encompassed in this building. It's a testament to the influential people that set their roots here. When the tour guide finishes showing us around, we thank him and go our separate ways.

'As this is a town popular for its hot springs and luxurious spas, how can we experience the city fully without visiting at least one spa?' I whisper into Yasmine's ear, and she jumps up and hugs me tightly.

'Yes, yes, yes. Let's go.'

Laughing, I hold her tight to me and gently lower her to the floor, laying a kiss on her lips. A kiss full of happiness and joy. We end up going to a well-known spa called Carolus Thermen Bad Aachen. It's what I expected and more. There are many baths, both ice cold (which is unsurprisingly empty as the weather is freezing) and warm baths that we relax in and have fun in for an hour. We come out looking fresh, and Yasmine can't stop smiling from ear to ear. A cab takes us to our next tour site, Altstadt. We find lots of information about Altstadt from a pamphlet we get from a stall upfront.

'Let me read it,' Yasmine says, and I hand it to her.

'Altstadt is Germany's old town, which has been preserved for decades to show people what cities and their lives were like back in the days. It has a lot of places like bars, dance clubs, and pubs. Museums here include the Schifffahrtsmuseum and the K20,' she reads this out loud as we stroll around the town.

'Let's go to the Schifffahrtsmuseum first.' I pull her closer to myself to avoid being separated by the crowd.

The Schifffahrtsmuseum displays the German naval fleet of World War 1. We see ship models, artwork, posters, and other artefacts. There are also a few historic ships tied up alongside the pier. Sadly, there's no tour available now, and we didn't book ahead of time. We take lots of pictures before moving to the K20. The K20 is a contemporary art display. It's the main gallery and has excellent collections of 20th century German Expressionism. There are some art displays from Picasso, Klee, Marc, and Kirchner.

'Let me take pictures of you,' Yasmine says as she gets the camera ready for picture taking. I gladly pose in front of various art displays, and she snaps away. She takes lovely pictures, but mine are better, and I tell her just as much, making her snort.

'You wish,' she laughs.

I take pictures of her, too, before we head out to the market stalls lining the street.

'I'm going to buy some things for Pearl, Cross, and Russ,' I announce, and she helps me pick out things that we think they'll like.

She picks out some stuff for her mum, Charlotte, and a few other friends I don't know. We catch sight of restaurants and pop in one to have a meal. The staff are polite and helpful, and the food is unfamiliar but delicious. We stroll around for a longer time, taking many pictures. A stranger takes some pictures of us too. Soon enough, it gets dark, and we decide to head back to the hotel.

'Let's walk back,' Yasmine suggests. 'We've been cooped up in vehicles too much.'

The walk is refreshing and takes no longer than 30 minutes. The street is still filled with people moving around, but we agree to call it a day, as we have more things to explore tomorrow. She bought some snacks from the market, so we sit down on the couch to eat them after a hot shower. I adamantly refused to share it with her, much to her disappointment. I recline on the couch and stretch my legs.

'Where am I to sit?' she questions.

'Right here,' I point to the space my legs have created, and she lowers herself and reclines on my chest.

My hand goes to her stomach, and I slip it under her shirt and start tracing circles on her stomach. We eat the snacks and make small talk. I clear my throat slightly, and her body turns slightly towards me.

'What's wrong?' she asks.

'I know this is not fancy and flashy, but it's special for me, and I hope it will be special for you too,' I start, 'Yasmine, since the first day I met you at the Louvre, I knew I wanted to be as close to your heart as possible. The short time we've spent together has shown me that you are better than I imagined. I've fallen in love with you, and I want you to be mine. Yasmine, please be my girlfriend.'

I don't know why I'm so nervous about this, but my heart is thumping, and I hope she doesn't notice. She detangles herself from me and turns to face me.

'Jace, you love me?'

'Yes, princess, I love you. I love the way you talk, your little smiles, your deep belly laughs and your enthusiasm for life.'

She's smiling so hard at this point, and I'm hopeful. She

leans forward and kisses me. My hand moves to her waist, and I drag her closer. Her happiness reflects in this kiss, and I don't want it to end.

'Yes, Jace, I'll be your girlfriend. I love you so much,' she announces with the biggest smile I've ever seen on her face.

My heart is soaring with happiness, and I hoot with joy and drag her back to kiss me. She settles herself on my lap, and we're so close that there's no space between our bodies. We pull back to catch our breaths, and she buries her face in my neck. I hug her tightly and kiss her head. Day 5 has been beautiful.

Yasmine drags me out of bed. 'Come on, sleepyhead.'

We slept very late last night as our talk carried us into the night. I'm still feeling like the last vestiges of sleep, but Yasmine has the clear and wide-eyed look of a baby.

Our first stop today is Dusseldorf Central Station, and it's about an hour away from here. When we get in the cab, I rest my head on Yasmine's shoulders and close my eyes a little. When her hand comes up to caress my cheeks, it makes me smile. The cab dropped us off at the station we used when coming from the Netherlands. We pay for a tour and a guide is assigned to us. He leads us to the entrance, where he begins his explanations.

'Dusseldorf Central Station or Düsseldorf Hauptbahnhof is the main railway station of Dusseldorf, the capital of North-Rhine Westphalia in Germany. There are 16 rails, four trams, and four stadtbahn.' He points his hand to show us the direction of the rails. 'Krüger and Eduard Behne are the architects that designed the station. They designed it in a New Objectivity architectural style, the modern architecture that took Europe by storm from the 1920s and 30s.'

We choose to stay in an area with lots of people because the last time we saw that thing was in a railway station, and the feeling of déjà vu is powerful here. The station is quite large, and we're shown its complete outline on paper. We finish the tour and thank the tour guide before moving out.

'According to this,' Yasmine looks at the itinerary in her hand, 'our next stop and the last for today is the Cologne Cathedral, which should be a few minutes away from here.'

'Before we go,' I reply, 'let's have a seat somewhere.'

We move to a restaurant that has enclosed seats. We choose the one that we think will give us more privacy. After ordering drinks, I turn to look at her.

'You remember we said that we'll tell each other something every day,' and she nods at this. 'This counts towards a secret,' I continue. 'The day Aiden died, I had a terrible dream. I dreamt I was in a beautiful forest with lush vegetation and towering trees. It was a beautiful place. Then my hand moved towards a little plant that was right in front of me. I plucked a leaf from the plant, and everything went to shit. The leaves turned brown and started falling in heaps, and the towering trees collapsed to the ground as if they'd been cut. The sky turned black. I couldn't see anything in front of me and felt like I was falling. I woke up in a sweat and pondered over the dream for a while, but I forgot about it and didn't tell anyone, as I couldn't make sense of it. If I had, I would have known that the dream meant that a single action of mine will lay waste to what was a beautiful thing.'

She scoots closer to me and hugs me tightly as I take in the scent of her skin to calm myself down.

'No need to beat yourself up over it,' she whispers into my ear.

I straighten up in my seat, and she clears her throat slightly before speaking.

'My freshman year in college, I got into a lot of trouble for throwing my shoe at a girl when she came into my dorm room to see my roommate, and the shoe hit her smack dab on her forehead. It was this heavy boot that I loved wearing, and she suffered a minor concussion. I gave no reason for my violence, as I had never met the girl in my life. The truth was, as soon as the door opened, I felt a chill in my bones. I was facing the opposite direction and turned to investigate the source of the cold. I saw a girl enter the room, but what scared me was the thing I saw standing behind her. It looked ashen and dry, with sunken holes where the eyes should have been. It was snarling with teeth that were falling out, and I panicked. Its hands extended towards the girl, and it looked like it was trying to touch her, so I aimed my shoe at it and threw, but I miscalculated, and the shoe hit the girl. I could tell no one what I saw as I didn't know myself what I had seen.'

We sit there for several long minutes and stew in our words. This thing hadn't begun now. There had always been signs of it, but we never understood.

'Alright. Let's head to the next place,' I say as I call for the bill.

After paying, we head out and get a cab to take us to our next destination, the Cologne Cathedral. After being dropped off, we walk up the entrance, and a priest lets us in quickly. The sheer size of this place is sickening. As many people are milling around, we merge in and find a group with a tour guide. The tour has already begun, but we're able to glean some information from them.

'The Cologne Cathedral located in Cologne, North-Rhine Westphalia, is the largest Gothic church in Germany. It was declared a World Heritage Site in 1996. Construction started on 15 August 1248, and the cathedral was finally opened on 27 September 1322. It was designed in the Gothic architecture style.'

There's a lot to see and enjoy in the cathedral. It feels so full of history and prayers it has heard for centuries. We move outside and take tons of pictures. The sky is darkening, so I drag Yasmine into a cab because I have plans for tonight.

'What's going on?' she asks indignantly. 'I wasn't done taking pictures.'

'We're going out for dinner tonight,' I say and then direct the driver, all the while aware of her surprised look.

'Wow. I didn't know,' she says with a soft smile.

We get to our room and get dressed in fancy clothes before heading out to the reservation I booked for us. We arrive at the restaurant and are shown to our table. The night is entertaining, with great food, fine wine, and slow music. When it's time to go, I'm thrilled we came.

Getting to the hotel room, Yasmine kisses me immediately. I close the door. We take off our clothes, and I stall her kisses long enough to take off her dress and shoes. She gets on the bed staring at me with those entrancing ice-blue eyes. My clothes follow suit, and I move up the bed, kissing my way up her body as I go. I take off her remaining clothes before parting her legs with my body and lean down to kiss her. As my mouth explores hers, my hands explore her body, going down until they touch the soft wetness that I had dreamed about all day. I swallow her moans and continue to feel her body. My other hand joins the first and moves up her body until I get to her breasts. Those gorgeous mounds practically beg for my attention. She writhes on the bed, and I still her movement with my body. Her hand creeps between us and massages me. The warmth of her palms, together with its softness, makes me groan into her mouth. My reaction fuels her enthusiasm, and she moves her hand, increasing her rhythm until I still her hands with mine. Reaching for the drawer, I get protection and wrap myself with it before suffocating myself in the warm heat of her body.

Day six was a dream. I smile in bed as memories of last night assail me, and I pull Yasmine's nude body closer to mine, making her stir in her sleep. She opens her eyes and smiles tiredly at me.

'Good morning, princess,' I smile back at her.

'Morning,' she leans forward to kiss me.

'You don't have to wake up early. We're only visiting one place today,' I tell her.

She goes right back to sleep, which makes me chuckle as I go to bathe and brush my teeth. Someone's tired. She wakes later in the morning, freshens up, and we head out for breakfast. There's a little cafe near our hotel which specialises in breakfast food. We have pancakes and syrup with coffee before heading out to start our tour. A cab takes us to Koln, where we visit a shop called Ullbara Western boots. The shop looks good with an assortment of shoes of every size, colour, and design.

'What do you say?' Yasmine says next to me, 'Are you buying some shoes?'

Hmm, I should. There are nice shoes here.

'Yeah, I am,' I reply, 'help me pick out shoes.'

We spend a long time perusing the shoes available, and I pick out a few. I also get a pair for each of my brothers, Russ and Cross. I think they'll like it. When we're done, we head outside to where there are shops selling anything and everything. There's a large crowd around us. I know it's strange, but I swear that someone is watching me. Looking at Yasmine, I see she is window shopping at a snack-selling shop, so it can't be her. I look around me, trying to figure out who is giving me this weird feeling. Yasmine notices my unease.

'What's wrong?'

'Someone is watching us,' I reply, and her forehead crinkles with worry.

She joins me to look around the busy street. I hear her gasp and grab hold of my hand.

'Jace, look. It's that woman, the store owner in Belgium.'

I look in the direction she's pointing and see a woman figure cloaked from head to toe, breaking into a run.

Chapter Six
Jace Tanner

I am finding it hard to believe that the creepy woman from Belgium would be here in Germany. Has she been following us? Or are we mistaking her for someone else? Well, there's one way to find out all this. Quickly, we break into a run after the figure, receiving a lot of looks from passers-by to whom we hurriedly apologise. We get to where we saw her, but it seems like she has escaped.

'Damn,' Yasmine exclaims, 'we've lost her in the crowd.'

'Not so fast,' I say as I peer carefully through a group of people in the distance.

It seems that everyone decided to wear the same colour jackets today, but I think I'm seeing someone who's trying too hard to fit in.

'Got her.' I lead the way as Yasmine follows behind me.

'What? Where?' She asks incredulously.

I point towards the group of people. 'Look over there. Everyone's walking unhurriedly yet brisk while she's practically running and trying to get in front of the group.'

We make our way through the crowd, and when she gets to a place with fewer people, she looks back and sees us following her. She runs again, but we're hot on her trails this time. The strange looks have turned to a look of open annoyance. We're practically sprinting through the street, and understandably, people are not too thrilled about it.

'Quick! She's turning into another street,' Yasmine

urges as the woman takes an immediate turn into another street. I hold Yasmine's hand.

'Wait, that street ends in a T-junction.' Two streets also flanked the street she took on either side. It appears that her street has no proper direction. Instead, it branches off into two alleys.

'Let's split up,' Yasmine suggests.

We take one alley each, getting to the end just in time to see the woman appear from the street she took. It seems she can't see us, so she takes the same alley as me. I merge with the crowd while I wait for her. When she gets within grasp, I shoot my hand out and grab hold of her upper arm while examining her face to find out her identity.

'So, it really is you?' I blurt out in shock. Her dirty hair and facial features are the same, and it's no wonder Yasmine identified her immediately after she saw her. I feel a light touch on my hand and look back to see that Yasmine has walked up to me.

'I mean no harm. Please,' the woman grunts as she fights to get out of my grip.

'Then why did you follow us from Belgium to Germany?' Yasmine asks as she stares fiercely at her.

'I don't think we should talk about it here,' I cut in suggestively. 'You're coming with us,' I proceed to tell her.

'Well, you're obviously not giving me a choice,' she replies, with not even a bit of unhappiness.

Shrugging, I stand by her right side, and Yasmine stands on her other side. We walk to the hotel with her sandwiched between us. We get to the hotel and unanimously agree to stay in the hotel's restaurant. When we sit down, with her in the middle, Yasmine speaks first.

'I know you already knew where we were staying. Am I right?'

The guilt-ridden look on the woman's face confirms our suspicion.

'I haven't been in here, if that's what you are wondering,' she replies. 'I just stop at the outskirts, that's all.'

'Why?' Just a one-word question from me, and she clams up.

Yasmine and I look at each other, trying to communicate through our facial expressions.

'I think you can do better than that,' Yasmine chimes in, and the woman's face flicks nervously to look at her before she lowers it to the table again. 'Okay, look, at least tell us your name first. Let's start from somewhere,' Yasmine says in a calm tone. She looks up at a spot in front of her and mumbles some incoherent words.

'What?' I strain to hear her. 'I didn't get that.'

'Agatha,' she clears her throat. 'I'm Agatha Jacobs.'

'Well, Agatha, I'm Jace.'

'And I'm Yasmine.'

'Can you explain what you are doing here in Germany?'

I ask, still maintaining the calm tone Yasmine used.

'I came for a tour of the city,' she says with a smile that looks forced.

'Mhm, mhm. Of course you did,' I murmur as Yasmine snorts on her other side.

'We're still waiting, Agatha,' Yasmine says, and she visibly exhales a breath of air as if bracing herself for something.

'Okay, I admit it. I have been trailing you,' she finally rushes out.

With our suspicions affirmed, Yasmine and I share similar looks of horror and surprise.

'You were with us at Amsterdam too?' Yasmine hesitantly asks, as if she fears the answer.

'Yes,' Agatha lowers her head shamefully, 'I was in the Netherlands, too.'

How did we not see her? How has she been following us for days without us noticing?

'Before you freak out, just listen,' Agatha continues, and at this statement, Yasmine looks incredulous.

'BEFORE we freak out?' I hear her ask Agatha with a slightly raised voice.

'Right,' Agatha replies, 'that was silly of me. Of course, you've already freaked out. I didn't plan to follow you two for all this time. I was only trying to protect you.'

This time around, I'm the one that speaks up, 'Protect

us from what?'

She turns to look at me with a blank expression. 'What has been happening that you need protection from?'

Yasmine gasps and raises her eyes to mine before turning to look at the woman.

'We should have known. You know something about what we have been seeing on this trip.'

'Yes, I do,' she murmurs, 'but listen to me first.' When we're quiet and staring at her expectantly, she starts explaining, 'You see, I knew something had gone wrong back in my shop. When I read your aura, I told you I could sense something wrong.' She looks at Yasmine now, and I remember what happened in her shop. From Yasmine's expression, I see she recalls it, too. 'I had seen that your aura was troubled. Evil forces are fighting for a chance. To do what? I don't know, but they were pretty intense, so I sought to conduct a spell to chase them from you. I switched my spell, from that of a simple aura check to a spell meant to chase away evil.' She turns to stare at us accusingly, 'But no! You wouldn't let me finish the spell. You don't know that a half-done spell is worse than no spell at all, and by cutting me off in the middle of the spell, the evil found its way to you.'

An audible gasp escapes Yasmine as the realisation hits us.

'So, you followed us? Why not warn us when we

were about to leave your shop?' I ask curiously, because why would she trail after us for so many days instead of immediately bringing it to our attention? A guilty look settles on her face.

'Well, I wasn't sure that you would see anything. You know things of that nature are usually met with a lot of scepticism, and you two looked sceptical already, so I was reluctant to tell you about it and had decided to do it by myself.' She's not lying. We doubted everything about her, and it's now evident that she can see it in our faces. She continues, 'I decided to trail you to convince myself that nothing was wrong, and I was being paranoid. It didn't work, though. I saw everything that happened in the Royal Museum of Fine Arts of Belgium.'

'You were in the museum too?' A shocked Yasmine asks.

'Yes,' she concurs, 'I went into the museum and watched you two from a distance. I saw you stare down the corridor and call your friend's attention to it, but he couldn't see it. When I sneaked behind you and acted like I was just another tourist walking past, I saw it too. That's when I knew I was right. The ghost had found its way to you.'

'Then what?' Yasmine questions, 'Why didn't you tell us then?'

'I don't know why I didn't call you two right away and break the news to you. I was just scared that you would blame me for it, so I decided to do it myself. I've been trying to get rid of the ghost for days now, but to no avail. It's tough to do so, with both of you being none the wiser. I had finally decided to tell you about it and enlist your help before you caught sight of me today.'

'What do you mean by enlisting our help?' Yasmine questions curiously, 'Because I don't see what we can do. I mean, this thing has scared us shitless out of our minds, whatever it may be.'

'What it is, my dear, is a ghost of a man impaled by Vlad the Impaler,' she replies, and the silence that ensues is deafening.

'If I hadn't seen this thing myself, I would laugh,' I say with equal feelings of amusement and shock.

'Vlad the Impaler? I don't understand. Is it the same Vlad the Impaler that was Vlad the third, Prince of Wallachia?' Yasmine queries.

'Yes,' Agatha answers, and Yasmine's tight face turns to mine before she turns it back to Agatha.

'Is this some kind of joke to you? We were being serious with you and thought you would do the same with us. What does a man that ruled part of Romania some 500 years ago have to do with what's happening now?' Yasmine questions.

'I knew you wouldn't believe me. This is exactly why I kept it to myself all this time,' Agatha says as she starts to stand up. 'I think it's time I took my leave.'

'No,' Yasmine puts her hand gently on Agatha's shoulder, 'please don't go yet.'

I try reasoning with her, 'Agatha, you should understand how this must sound to us. First, we have been seeing ghosts, and now you're saying that it's a ghost of one of the people who died hundreds of years ago by a man famous for his brutal acts. Surely you can see how insane that sounds?'

She sits down and looks away from us. 'I do realise that I don't sound very plausible, but…' she turns to Yasmine, 'when you first saw the ghost, what did you notice?'

Yasmine stares at her quietly before I see her face light up.

'The most prominent thing I noticed was that he had some type of stick stuck in his stomach, and I thought it was a trick of the light.'

I feel my eyes widen as the realisation dawns on me that Yasmine is right. Agatha turns to look at me with an expression that says, 'See, see.'

'Yasmine,' Agatha turns back to Yasmine, 'you know a lot of historical stuff, right?'

'Yes,' Yasmine chuckles a bit.

'Then you should know about how Vlad the third killed.'

'Yes, I do,' Yasmine clears her throat. 'Vlad the third

was a prince of Wallachia and ruled three times. His last rule was in 1476. His moniker "The Impaler" was given to him because he enjoyed killing his victims by impaling them on stakes. He impaled about 20,000 men and killed a total number of about 60,000 people in his short rule. To impale them, he put a stake through them, and it's often said that he left the men hanging on those stakes for days. A rather horrible way to die.'

'Wow,' that's all I can say right now. My mind is a tumbled-up affair.

'Yes indeed, wow,' Agatha replies. 'Vlad the Impaler killed people by… well,' she chuckles nervously, 'impaling them, and the ghost you've been seeing is one of the men impaled by Vlad the third. He is determined to follow you both.'

We turn at once to stare at her because what in the world could be funny about this entire issue?

'Don't look at me like that,' Agatha admonishes us. 'From what I've found out, when these men were impaled, few refused to proceed to the underworld. They have been waiting at the berth between life and death, waiting for an opportunity to come back to earth. They have been roaming around for hundreds of years, and yes, something had to have happened before they found out about you.'

'What could have happened to make them know us?' I ask, confused.

'Think back. Did you perhaps meddle in the occult? Or anything that had to do with messing with spirits and the likes? Only something of that nature could have drawn them to you,' Agatha replies.

'Oh! Shit,' Yasmine quietly exclaims.

'What?' I ask. 'Do you remember something?'

'Yes, Jace, I do,' Yasmine replies and looks at me. 'Do you remember the secrets we told each other days ago of when we were younger?' she asks, and my heart skips a beat.

It can't be, can it? Is it possible that those things we did as foolish kids could be the cause of all this? Agatha's face is flitting expectantly between our faces, trying to gauge the reason for our reactions.

'These things happened when we were younger, and since then, we haven't had any encounters with spirits,' I say to Agatha, but she scoffs.

'Tell me what happened, and I'll know if it's the cause or not.'

'Okay,' I begin, 'when I was younger, I went to a woman who owned a shop that looked a lot like yours. She was new to town and quite strange, but I went there because I had a peculiar request. I asked her if she could make me see or speak to my late brother, who had died before I was born, and she said yes.' Taking a deep breath, I continued, 'She did some things I still don't understand,

and I was terrified of being found out by my parents. I don't know when I fainted, but when I woke up later, I was still where I had been sitting, and I couldn't see the woman, so I ran out of her shop. That's all that happened.'

After I finish recounting my experience, Yasmine starts to describe hers.

'The only experience of an occult nature that I can think of is something I had thought to be a creepy teenage experience.' She shuffles on her seat before she continues her explanation. 'There was a girl in middle school who proclaimed that she could see ghosts, and this made her look somehow cool in our eyes. So, I befriended her, and she invited me to a sleepover at her place. When we were there, I asked her to make me see ghosts too, and she agreed. During the process, I felt weirded out just like I felt during yours,' she looks at Agatha, 'so I told her I was feeling creeped out and asked her to stop.'

When she pauses, Agatha urges her on. 'Yes, what happened next?'

'She objected and said that she'll have to complete the process or there'll be consequences. I didn't listen and brushed it off as a silly game teen girls play at sleepovers. We didn't speak that night, and I remember that we barely spoke until her family moved away from the town. That's all that happened.'

Agatha seems to think for some time before turning

to me.

'Jace, I don't know what exactly happened, but what I think is that the woman you went to was a big fake. She didn't know what to do and stopped halfway, leaving you exposed to these ghosts.' She then turns to Yasmine. 'In your case, it's quite clear that the girl was not bluffing. You know she wanted to make you see ghosts, but she didn't get to complete things. She was supposed to do the first spell that would make you immune to the ghosts. They weren't supposed to come after you or trail you. Only then would she have completed the second spell that would make you see and communicate with them, but she rather did the opposite. She was about to complete the second as first, and only then did she plan to do the first. That's when you told her to stop. This opened you to the ghost, but they couldn't appear to you because she held them back by not completing the second spell.' We sit shell shocked by this information. She speaks to Yasmine, 'When you came to my shop, remember I was looking at your aura, and I said that there's a lot of negative energy around you? I tried to get rid of it, thinking it was something smaller. But you two got freaked out and asked to go. The ghosts were halfway out of the barrier of the human world. They were desperately fighting to get inside and make their way to you, their humans. When I opened the barrier to push them inside, they were stronger than I had expected, and that's when I suspected that these were more than normal negative energies. I switched my spell to a stronger spell, and if you were observant, you would have noticed that. That's when you insisted I stop the spell, and as you two were adamant on leaving, I wished hard that my assessment was wrong and that it was nothing more than normal negative energies. I was wrong, and that's why we're here.'

'So that's why this thing has been after us?' Yasmine quietly says.

'This thing?' Agatha asks, looking surprised. 'You do know two ghosts are trailing after you and not just one, right?'

'What?'

'No way!' We exclaim at once.

'Oh yes, there are two ghosts. One for each of you,' she laughs nervously, and upon seeing our stony expressions, she quietens. 'They look alike because they are from the same era and therefore dressed similarly. Besides, I'm sure their looks are too scary for you to focus on their faces,' she explains, and this makes me understand everything.

'So, what do you suggest we do now?' Yasmine asks.

'What I want us to do is quite simple as long as you follow my instructions.' She pauses dramatically. I've noticed that she's a bit on the dramatic side. 'We need to trap them,' she drops, and it seems like we didn't hear her correctly. Because who's we?

'We? Trap who?' Yasmine questions.

'You heard me. I know you did,' Agatha replies.

'Of course, we heard you,' Yasmine continues, 'the problem is that I don't trust what I heard.'

'What do you mean by WE have to trap them?' I question.

'The reason I've been unable to come in contact with these ghosts is that they are attached to you. They come out and show themselves to you and maybe anyone you're with. All my trials in invoking them have been null and void, as only you two can make them come out.'

'But we don't know what makes them come out,' I argue.

'Yes, but there are ways we can attract them to come out. When they're comfortable enough, I can chase them back to the underworld.'

'How will we know they're comfortable enough?' Yasmine questions.

'When they think you are powerless and at their mercy. They always have their guards up and trying to deal with them at this stage will erupt in a fatal fight. They need to think that their links to the real world can not oppose them, and that's when I'll strike,' Agatha explains.

This revelation leaves a foul taste on my tongue because it means that these ghosts have to harm us physically before she can send them away.

'No,' I say when I see that Yasmine's fearful and questioning eyes are fixed on mine.

She, too, has realised what Agatha meant by us looking vulnerable to the ghosts. It means they might harm us or, worse still, kill us before Agatha can act. Besides, what's the guarantee that she can face these ghosts? What if she's just bluffing and the spirits make snacks out of the three of us?

'Isn't there another way for us to do this without offering ourselves as some sort of human bait?' Yasmine asks, and Agatha shakes her head from side to side.

'No, there's no other way. Nothing else will make them relaxed enough to let their guards down.'

'We can't do that, Agatha. Let's find another way, please,' I beg, and Agatha looks torn.

'I don't know another way we can go about this,' Agatha replies, 'but why exactly do you not want to do it?'

I exchange glances with Yasmine, contemplating if we should tell her or not.

'Look, Agatha,' Yasmine begins, 'please don't take offence to this, but you're basically asking us to put ourselves in harm's way, trusting that you will save us.'

'But that's the problem,' I add. 'we don't trust you enough for that. We barely know you, and this seems like a journey of no return if we do this.'

Agatha's face is scrubbed of emotions. I hope I have not

hurt her feelings, but we're just trying to keep ourselves safe. 'I understand,' she finally replies.

'You do?' Yasmine asks, with surprise written all over her face.

'Yes, I do,' Agatha confirms, 'the only other alternative is for me to keep on trying to summon them by myself, but it's proving to be very difficult. I'll find a way, though. Even I know that what I'm asking you to do is insanely dangerous. Those ghosts are maniacal and won't hesitate to kill you. I don't even know what exactly they want with you, but it's safe to assume that they're out for blood.'

Seeing that the conversation has reached a lull, I request water from the waiters, which they quickly bring.

'So, what now?' I ask.

'Now, you continue your holiday, but please keep in touch with me.'

'Are you going back to Belgium?' Yasmine questions her.

'No, my conscience won't let me go back home to Belgium, leaving you at the mercy of those things. I'll come with you until we're sure that we've got rid of them.'

'Okay, then I'll get tickets for you to come with us...' I say, but she cuts me off.

'I would appreciate that, but please, I can't be seen with you again. As it is, I've spent too much time with you, and if the ghosts make an appearance and see me with you, they won't willingly come out for a very long time.'

'So, I'll just get you tickets but in another cabin from us, and I'll book hotel rooms for you until we're done,' I say, but then something comes to my mind. 'Which reminds me of something. Agatha, where have you been staying in the different countries we've visited?'

An embarrassed flush rises to her cheeks.

'I've been staying with some friends who are in the same line of business as I am. They are more than happy to take me in.'

'Will you be okay staying in a hotel room, different hotels to us but still within walking distance?' Yasmine inquires.

'Yes, that would be quite all right,' she replies, and I smile in relief. At least that's taken care of now.

We accompany her to a hotel a few blocks from ours, where I pay in advance for her room. Once we're done with that, we go outside to talk.

'I'll head over to my friend's place to grab my things, then I'll come back here. And before you ask, no, I don't want to come with you on your tours. I'll focus on trying to get rid of this thing while you two get your money's worth.'

'That's quite alright, dear,' Yasmine replies, 'but can we have your phone number? You know, in case of emergencies.'

She agrees, and we exchange phone numbers before we

head back to our room.

'Wait, Jace, what's she going to eat? You know she's here because of us,' Yasmine asks, haltering her steps.

'I've taken care of that,' I assure her 'it's part of the services the hotel renders. She'll get breakfast, lunch, and dinner.'

'Wow!' she exclaims gleefully. 'That was so sweet of you, but I insist on paying for our meal today.' At my confused look, she explains. 'It's just my way of saying that I appreciate what you did today for her.'

I hug her in the middle of the street. 'You're welcome, princess.'

As the sky darkens, we head to the hotel and request dinner in the lobby. We eat, and she pays before we go upstairs to sleep away the stress of the day.

7 DAYS TO CHRISTMAS

18 December 2008

'Hurry up, slugger head,' Yasmine cajoles.

'How do you come up with these names?' I wonder out loud.

'Well, my dear boyfriend,' she skips over to where I'm standing, 'it's a gift of mine. Now hurry. The day has gone quick.'

Chuckling, I walk over to her and stand behind her to wrap my arms around her waist.

'Well, dear girlfriend of mine, I don't know where you get such energy from in the morning, but I'm still sleepy-eyed.'

She giggles at this, and I lower my lips to her neck and lay gentle kisses on the side of her neck. She tilts her neck to the side to give me more access as little sighs of pleasure escape her lips.

'What do you say? Should we take a break from sightseeing today and stay in the hotel room?' I murmur, mesmerised by the softness of her skin, but she only laughs.

Turning around in my arms to face me, she stands on her tiptoes and places her lips on mine.

'Nope,' she pulls back to say, 'we have plans today. When we're back, I'll kiss you as much as I want.' Well, I can't object to that.

We get dressed and head out of the hotel room and into the rapidly approaching sunrise. And no, it's not that early. The time is 11.30am, and it has been raining cats and dogs since this morning. The rain just decided to bid us farewell, for now, so we make use of this opportunity to rush out and explore more of Germany. Peering at the itinerary, I see as

Yasmine's brows furrow adorably. I'm just happy she's not looking too affected by what transpired yesterday. As I'm looking at her, she suddenly lifts he heads up.

'It appears we're going to the…' she looks again at the itinerary, 'Galeria Kaufhof first,' she pronounces carefully. 'I'm definitely saying it wrong, but that's the best I can do for now,' she adds while laughing.

Where we're heading is within walking distance, so we stroll casually to it, skipping through the puddles of water on the streets and navigating the crowd.

'The Galeria Kaufhof is a department store,' Yasmine reads again from the itinerary.

'That means we'll get a lot of shopping done,' I add. It makes sense, I guess.

I have to buy more things for Russ and Cross and some bags for Pearl. She does love bags. When we get to the imposing structure, there are groups of people waiting for a tour guide, so we pay and are quickly allocated to a group. Soon, a young woman comes and introduces herself as our guide.

'Galeria Kaufhof is a German department store chain with its headquarters in Cologne, which you may know as Köln. A man named Leonhard Tietz, a German merchant with Jewish origins, opened it in 1879. It currently employs over 17,000 people and serves Germany and Belgium.'

She leads us around the stories of buildings that make

up the department store. It appears anything can be found here, as there are tons of shops selling everything imaginable. When the tour is over, everyone thanks her, and we say our goodbyes as she leaves. This store is very extensive, and we want to take our time to go through it. Many outfits and show trials later, we have managed to buy a good number of things. I have found three bags for Pearl that Yasmine tells me are in good taste and look fashionable. I got Yasmine's mum's gift and some nice belts and cufflinks for Russ and Cross. As I pay for the gifts, my mind slips to Cross, and I wonder how he's doing. Calls are not allowed when inside the rehabilitation centre, and only one person can visit you. That person is Russ, and only he can tell me how Cross is doing. I'll make sure to call him tonight. Yasmine's voice intercepts my thoughts.

'Hey, babe, what do you think of this bag?'

I look to see her holding a brown bag that I'm sure she picked from the men's section. I saw it but only when I'd picked lots of other things for everybody. I didn't think it would be a good idea to buy this one and disregarded myself.

'It looks nice,' I comment, and it really does look good.

'Okay,' she chirps, then puts it into her bag.

Hmm, what's she doing with a man's bag? I decide that maybe it's for a friend, before continuing to peruse the shop.

'Are you hungry, princess?' I ask a preppy-looking Yasmine.

'Yes, I think the restaurants are on the other side,' she points towards the next floor.

We move there to see an assortment of restaurants, all selling different things.

'We've had a lot of German food since we arrived. I'm in the mood for French food,' Yasmine grumbles as she catches sight of a French restaurant.

'Whatever you say, Mademoiselle,' I dramatically bow in her direction.

'Stop that,' she laughs and runs over to me.

Laughing, I straighten myself before moving to the restaurant where we sit down to have our meal. When we're done, we pay and head out of the store and into the street, where we spend hours watching the roadside plays put on by different groups, who are all celebrating the holidays and the cheer it brings. When the sky has darkened, with the nightlights being the only thing illuminating the streets, we make our way cheerfully back to the hotel.

'I'm too full for dinner,' Yasmine comments, and I wholeheartedly agree. As well as the lunch we had at the Galeria Kaufhof, we'd eaten plenty of snacks and street food today, so it's no surprise that we're full. Remembering that I have calls to make, I excuse myself and head to the couch to call Pearl first. When the call connects, and she picks up, I can hear voices in the background.

'Hi, Pearl.'

'Hiya, Jace, how are you doing?'

'I'm doing great, sis. It seems you're busy over there.'

She laughs into the phone, 'yes, that's right. There's just a little party that's been held, and it turned out to be not so little.'

I laugh because I know precisely how parties seem to grow on their own.

'Why don't you have fun? We'll talk tomorrow,' I say, deciding to let her get back to the party.

'Of course. Wait, Jace,' she says as I'm about to disconnect the call. 'Have you called Russ?' I hear the laughter in her voice instantly replaced by a hard edge, and my palms turn sweaty. Has something, anything, happened to Cross?

'No, I plan on calling him once I end this call.'

'Okay, do so, please,' she says and disconnects the call just as I call out.

'Wait, Pearl, what's hap...?' I trail off when I realise that the line is silent.

The room seems silent, too, and I turn to see Yasmine seated on the bed, looking anxiously at me. It's safe to say she heard the call and found it weird, too. I dial Russ's line, and he doesn't pick at first, so I try again, and he picks on the third ring.

'Hey, bro,' his tired voice comes through the line.

'Hi, Russ,' I reply, 'how have you been doing?'

'I've been good, and I got a job last week at this company. I'm not exactly sure what I'm supposed to do, but I'll learn on the job.'

We laugh at this. If there's one thing that Russ is good at, it's learning fast. It's kind of his superpower. I decided to ask the dreaded question, 'How is Cross?'

A tired sigh escapes Russ's lips.

'I went to visit him today, and Jace, it's not going well.'

Dread fills my stomach.

'What's going on, Russ? He was okay when you went to visit him more than a week ago.'

'He relapsed, Jace. He has had a fucking relapse. They've placed him in an isolated room to stop him from hurting himself in his search for drugs of any kind. The anti-depressants that a nurse brought to him were the drug he wanted. When the nurse brought it in, he attempted to wrestle her and snatch the entire jar from her when he was supposed to only take two tablets.'

Fuck no, no, no. This is not good.

'Did he hurt the nurse?' I ask, dreading the coming reply.

'No, the security guards positioned at the doors came and detangled him from her, but he was so angry. He upturned the bed and everything in the room,' Russ replies.

'When I went there today, I was only allowed to speak to him through the door, and man, he fucking begged me for drugs.'

'How long does he have to stay there? Ten months?' I ask hopefully.

'Yes, that's the only good thing. We should have hope that he'll get better as long as he's there,' Russ affirms.

We say our goodbyes and end the call. After sitting for many minutes with my thoughts running a mile a minute, I decide to get ready for sleep.

'Why don't we freshen up, and then you can rest?' Yasmine suggests. She looks so worried, and going by the conflicted look in her eyes, it seems like she's debating something.

'Okay, princess, why don't you go ahead?' I say as I decide to let her finish first.

When Yasmine is done using the bathroom, I go in to freshen up, only to come back out to see the bag she bought in the shop lying on the bed. She sits beside it with glowing eyes.

'Princess,' I call, 'what's this?'

'It's a gift for you,' she says sweetly. 'I noticed you didn't get much for yourself today, so I got you this.'

To say I'm surprised is an understatement. She has got me gifts before, but this one just hits differently because of how terrible I feel after my call with Russ. It feels good to know that someone aside from my family cares about me enough to notice when I don't take good care of myself. I walk up to her as she stands up from the bed and envelope her in a hug, letting my nose breathe in her scent.

'Thank you, princess. I love it.'

'You're welcome, baby.' She curls her body into mine, and we just stay that way for a long moment.

When we finally get into bed, she lays her head on my chest and traces circles on my stomach. My mind wanders in thought while my body relishes in her warmth.

'Why don't we trade secrets to take your mind off what happened?' she suggests, and I wholeheartedly agree with her. She clears her throat. 'I'll go first. As a child, I always loved reading and being in the library, so I decided to be a librarian as they get to read all the books there.' We laugh, and she lay down more securely on me before continuing. 'One particular day, I retreated into a corner that's hard to find in the library and lost myself in a book. It was dark out by the time I looked up, but I still heard movement out front, so I thought I was still safe. I leisurely walked to place the book back in its spot before making my way out. It turns out the noise I had heard was the security guard making his first rounds for the night. The librarians had long gone home, and I was locked inside the library. Bear in mind, I was 14 and didn't have a phone yet, so all I could do was yell, but I didn't get anyone's attention.'

She sits up to look me in the eye. 'Babe, I stayed there for hours. I sat down on a couch and waited for my mum to find me before I remembered I had lied to her about my whereabouts. I was supposed to be at a friend's house, but I decided the library would be better and took a detour on my way to her house. The library was quiet at first, with only the light from the window illuminating everywhere. Then the temperature dropped, and I began to see a figure and what looked to be a human in the shadows. I thought it was my fear acting up, but it got real, and a hand draped in a long cloth extended out of the shadows. I screamed as I'd never screamed. Luckily for me, my mum, grandmum, and friend's mum searched for me and decided to try the library. They were speaking to the guard when they heard my scream and brought me out. I didn't tell anybody about the incident.'

She lies on my body, and I run my hands through her hair.

'Mine is brief but scary, nonetheless,' I begin. 'After that incident at the soothsayer's shop, the nights following it were littered with strange dreams. The most prominent dream is that I saw a strange baby still wearing its diaper talking to me. I don't remember exactly what was said, but I remember it lifted its hands to hug me. I screamed and woke up because what baby talks that well? The next day, I saw that same baby in my family's photo, and my mum told me it was my baby brother. I refused to sleep in my room for days and slept in Pearl's room.'

'We had very creepy childhoods,' Yasmine replies, and that makes me laugh because it's nothing but the truth.

Yasmine Belmont

6 DAYS TO CHRISTMAS
19 December 2008

'Today, we have engaging activities,' Jace announces as we eat on the balcony of our room. The weather is very encouraging today, and it seems we're going to take full advantage of it. I only hope it doesn't start raining later as the snow is not too thick today.

'Really? What first?' I ask through a mouthful of pancake.

'We're going to the Nürburgring first,' he says excitedly.

'Ooh, I've heard so much about this Nürburgring. It's high time I saw it,' I add, equally excited.

When we're done eating, we dress up and head out to start the day. We get a taxi to drive us to our destination and pay him before heading inside.

'Should we make use of a tour guide, or do you know

a little about here?' he questions.

'Yes, I know about this place, so there's no need for a tour guide.' When we get close enough to see the tracks, I explain, 'Nürburgring is a Motorsports complex in the town of Nürburg, here in Germany. Its construction began on 1st July 1925, and it was said to be the first German mountain, racing, and test road. It was officially opened on 18th June 1927 and currently has a capacity of 150,000 people. Major events held here include the Formula 1 race, German Grand Prix, European Grand Prix, Luxembourg Grand Prix, Eiffel Grand Prix, and others. This place has been the venue for some of the most important Formula 1 races in history.' I conclude my explanation to his resounding applause, and several heads turn to look at us.

'That was good,' he compliments.

'Thank you, but I don't think it will host any important races today,' I say as I observe the crowd that is nowhere near the size of the crowd at big races. It turns out that I'm right. When we get to the track, we find out that there is no official race, but anyone with a car can drive their vehicle through the track. Since we haven't got vehicles, we just stand on the sides to cheer on others who are racing, and take lots of pictures.

'Come on, let's go back to the hotel so we can get ready for the next location,' Jace urges me.

Wait, back to the hotel for what? He must see the

question on my face because he replies.

'We're going clubbing tonight.' I immediately jump up and down in happiness, not minding the crowd.

We go back to our room, have an early dinner, and I start getting ready. I'm so lucky that I packed clothes for every occasion. I choose a tight red grown with simple straps that shows a lot of cleavage. As it's very short and the nights are cold, I wear black tights with it and my heeled boots. Jace is dressed in long black trousers and a blue shirt, paired with a black jacket decorated with spikes. He looks like a rockstar, looking so good it's almost sinful. The taxi takes us to what we find out is called the Starfish Nightclub, in Aachen. It's a booming, filled up place complete with bars and a big dancefloor. The energy in the club is high, and before we know it, we're downing a couple of shots and moving to the dancefloor. I'm not the best dancer, but I know what to do. When we get to the dancefloor, it doesn't seem to matter because there's less dancing here and more jumping, depending on the song choice. It's a great song, and Jace and I dance freely around, laughing throughout. Jace constantly chases off advances from men who come to dance with me. I laugh so hard at this, but my laughter disappears when a brunette girl with huge boobs and extra dramatic makeup comes to rub herself on Jace's body. I move in between them and plaster myself to him, to the sound of his laughter. When the girl pouts and walks away, Jace puts his hand under my chin. When I'm staring up at him, he leans down and kisses me deeply.

'Is someone jealous?' I scoff at this and try to avert my eyes, but he directs them back to his. 'No need to be jealous. You're the only one I see. No one else matters.'

When we head back to the hotel, it's 2am, and we're exhausted. We take off our clothes before slipping into bed and fall asleep immediately.

5 DAYS TO CHRISTMAS

20th December 2008

I wake up in a freezing room. 'Babe, did you turn the heating off?' I question groggily. However, Jace is deeply asleep next to me. I check the little clock on the bedside table to see that it's only 5am and I attempt to go back to sleep when something catches my eye. Dread curls in my stomach as I turn fully behind me to see what it is.

'JACE!' I scream as I jump out of bed, and a perplexed Jace wakes up and jumps up with me.

His eyes run over the room before following my gaze,

and I feel his hand move immediately to my clenched fist. There, in the darkness, are two half-decayed, impaled ghosts, staring straight at us through their almost rotten eyes. It's true what Agatha said. There are two ghosts, but they look very alike, and it would be difficult to tell them apart. Jace's hand on mine tightens. One of the ghosts notices as its eyes move abruptly to our joined hands before moving back to our faces.

'Yasmine,' Jace whispers, 'RUN!'

We run to the locked door, and Jace wrenches it open in record time. We don't look back. I feel a hand grip my clothes, and I let out a scream, but Jace drags me forward, and I feel my clothes ripping. When we make it to the hallway, my screams seize, but we keep on running until we make it to the lobby, where the security rushes forward in haste.

'Ma'am, sir, what's wrong?' he queries urgently.

'Yes, please, there's…' I start to say, but Jace squeezes my hand

'No, sir. We just want to sit here in the lobby. Our room is incredibly stuffy,' he lies smoothly, and the security guard looks confused for a minute before shrugging his shoulders.

'That's alright with me,' he retreats to his post, and we sit down some distance away from him, but still close enough to the door.

'Why didn't you let me tell him?' I ask curiously.

'What do you think would have happened?' he replies. 'There are only two options. One, he calls us lunatics or alerts the manager that we may be mentally unsound because ghosts don't exist. The second option is, what if he magically believes that there are people in our room and goes in to check? Those things may kill him. We don't need anyone dead.'

Oh my God, that is true. I didn't stop to think that he wouldn't believe us.

'Let's call Agatha,' Jace suggests.

I remind him that our phones are in the room, and as we're both out of suggestions, we sit there in the lobby until it's bright outside. People have begun to come out of their rooms, and the security man is starting to look at us strangely.

'Let's go in and pack our bags, Yasmine. We're out of here,' Jace instructs, and we walk to our room with our heart in our throat. The door is still as wide open as we left it, and we stand at the entrance to peer intently into the room. 'Okay, it's clear,' Jace says. We rush into the room and start packing our bags.

'Quick. Go bathe,' Jace instructs as he takes over packing the bags.

I bathe the fastest I ever have and go in to see if Jace is done packing.

'Call Agatha and inform her of what's happened,' he calls out on his way to the bathroom.

When he comes out, I have finished a hurriedly made call to Agatha, who'll be meeting us at the train station. We grab our bags and hightail it out of the hotel room. We get a taxi, which takes us to Köln Hauptbahnhof, which is Köln's central station. I already purchased the tickets, and we show them before we're allowed onto the train. As we're proceeding inside, I catch sight of Agatha a few feet behind us in the line. I also got a good seat for her, so she'll be in the same compartment as us. The train ride from Köln Hauptbahnhof stops at Dresden Hauptbahnhof, where we change trains. From here to Prague's central station takes about two hours and before we know it, we've arrived at the Praha hlavní nádraží train station. The ride took over eight hours, and I'm relieved to be done with it. Another taxi takes us to our hotel just as Agatha's taxi takes her past us. Her hotel is a few blocks from ours, as she requested.

When we are shown to our room, I look fearfully around the room, trying to assure myself that there's nothing there. When I have looked everywhere and can't find anything, I sprawl tiredly on the bed.

'Should we stay in and rest today?' Jace asks from his place next to me on the bed.

'I don't know,' I moan tiredly. 'I'm just hungry.'

'I know, let's go feed you.' He stands from the bed and

reaches for my hand.

'Wait a minute, where are we supposed to visit today?' I ask as my curiosity overpowers my tiredness.

'Just the Sedlec Ossuary and the Charles Bridge.'

I yelp for joy and rush to put on my coat. 'Jace, we need to visit them today,' I say in between, putting on my coat.

His laughter gets to me. 'I knew you would love the Sedlec Ossuary.'

'Oh, I've read so much about it,' I exclaim with excitement. It feels like I'm bursting at the seams.

We hail a taxi that takes us to Kutná Hora, where the chapel is located. Upon getting there, to say I'm awed is an understatement. We proceed inside after paying for the tickets, and I see Jace's face turn pale with shock.

'Didn't you read about it first?' I ask, concerned about his reaction.

'Reading about it and seeing it are two different things, princess.'

'Okay, I'm sorry. Just keep in mind that these are all dead people's bones.' I take his arm, and he pulls my arm into the crook of his elbow.

'Okay, Miss historical conversationist. Please start explaining.'

I smile and tell him what I know about the place. 'First, you should know that an ossuary is a chest, building, or any site that serves a purpose as the final resting place of human skeletons. They are used when there's limited space for burials.'

We get to the infamous chandelier, and my mouth drops open in surprise at this macabre work of art. I close my mouth and assemble my thoughts to continue.

'Sedlec Ossuary is a Catholic chapel located beneath the Cemetery Church of All Saints. The Sedlec Ossuary contains approximately 40,000 to 70,000 human skeletons and the bones have been artistically arranged to form decorations. That chandelier is made entirely of bones, and skulls are draped all over it.'

There's a sound of awe from him, and it explains exactly what I'm feeling. We continue on to another part.

'Also executed in bones are those piers, a coat of arms which we're looking at now and the signature of František Rint.' We walk to where a signature is designed from bones. This is when we remember that we came with a camera, and Jace starts taking pictures of everything. 'Frantisek Rint was the Czech woodcarver employed to organise the human bones at the chapel. It became a UNESCO World Heritage Site in 1995.'

When we've taken pictures of everything possible, we move to gaze at the walls. Touching is forbidden and thank God for that. These things wouldn't have lasted that long if people could run their hands all over them. When we're done, we move out and, as we're both starving, we stop by a roadside restaurant that looks promising. We get an early dinner, and although some food items are unrecognisable, we enjoy our meal immensely. After resting for many minutes, we get up to continue our tour and take a taxi to Charles Bridge, which is about an hour away, based on the information we received from the restaurant owner. Even from a distance, it's clear that the Charles Bridge is an imposing structure.

'We will have to get a tour guide. I know little about the Bridge,' I announce.

When we get there, we find out that there's no paid tour guide available, and I'm at a loss.

'What are we going to do?'

'Hello, my dears,' a voice calls out behind us, and we turn to see a middle-aged woman.

'Hello ma'am,' we reply.

'I overheard you lamenting about the lack of a tour guide, but that rarely exists here. I'm a local and would be glad to show you around.'

We're so grateful, and she leads us to begin the tour.

'Charles Bridge is a medieval stone arch bridge that crosses the Vltava River in Prague, Czech Republic. It acts as a landmark and links towns. Its construction started in 1357 under King Charles IV and was completed in the early 15th century. The Charles Bridge replaced the old Judith Bridge that was built between 1158 and 1172.

The flood of 1342 badly damaged the old Judith Bridge. The Charles Bridge was originally called Stone Bridge, or Kamenný. In our language, it was also called Prague Bridge or Pražský, but was formally changed to Charles Bridge many years later.'

She points out a lot of statues on the Bridge, telling us the history of each. In total, there are thirty statues, and she takes her time to explain each one to us. When the tour is done, we insist on paying her, but she rejects and looks insulted by it.

'Okay, ma'am. How about we buy you a cup of tea?' I suggest, and she thankfully agrees to this.

There are little shops everywhere, seemingly unbothered by the cold, dreary weather.

'Since it's almost dark, I would suggest you stay here until the sky has darkened. That's when you'll get to enjoy an amazing view,' she says before finishing up her cup of tea, and we take turns to give her hugs before she heads out.

We head out too to explore the little shops lining the street. We find stalls that sell hand-crafted jewellery, and I purchase many of them; some for me, some for mum, and some for Charlotte. Soon, it's dark, and we can now see what she was talking about. We go to a vantage point on the Bridge, and it looks like an explosion of colours has taken place. All the buildings are illuminated, and we can see the imposing structure of the Prague castle from here. I feel a gaze on me and turn to look at Jace, who is staring at me.

'What's wrong?' I ask, smiling softly. He looks so good under the lights, like a Christmas wish come true.

'Nothing,' he replies. 'I just feel blessed to have you standing beside me.'

My heart melts and I move close to him. Just as I stand on my tiptoes to kiss him, he leans down, and our lips meet in an explosion of feelings as intense as the lights shining at us. I love him so much.

'Let's go back to the hotel,' he whispers, and I wholeheartedly agree.

We get a taxi, which drops us at our hotel, and once we get to our room, he stands at the door and looks at me reverently. He moves towards me and stands before me, still looking at me in that particular way.

'I love you so much,' he says softly, and without waiting for me to say a word, his lips descend to mine. Before long, I'm lost in a feeling of pleasure so intense, one that Jace alone can give me.

Lying down with him behind me on the bed, I feel a peace I haven't felt in forever. I don't know what it is, but our spirits click together in a way that even I don't understand. I don't understand it, but I don't want it to end either.

'Do you have a secret to share with me?' he says as his fingers idly trace patterns on my naked skin.

'Yes, I do. The thing is,' I begin, 'I've never wanted to get married to anyone.'

'Never?' he asks.

'Never,' I confirm. 'When all other girls would dream about being in danger and getting saved by a handsome Prince Charming, I never dreamed or imagined that. My dream was to be in danger, and then somehow I'd get magical powers, save myself and come home to my mum.'

Jace laughs behind me, and I join him because, yes, it's funny.

'Does it have to do with your parent's failed marriage?' he asks, hitting the nail on the head.

'Yes, it does. My parent's marriage was like a fairy tale. A loving family and a beautiful life. Oh, how I adored my parent's marriage. How could something so beautiful turn so nasty and dangerous? It surprised and shocked me, and I concluded that marriages are not real. Because if my parent's love was not strong enough, whose love will be?' Taking a deep breath, I continued, 'As I grew up, I changed my mindset and resolved to give myself a chance and not summarise my life based on my parent's. But the people

I've given chances to have let me down, continuously, until I wondered if my younger self was correct?'

When I'm done speaking, he holds me tight.

'And now?' He nervously asks, and I feel his body tighten as he prepares himself for my answer.

I laugh at his nervousness. 'Now, I know my younger self was just scared. I'm going to give it a chance. Give everything a chance.'

I feel his body loosen from what I'm sure is a relief. He places a kiss on my neck before he speaks.

'I've never been in love,' he blurts out, and I turn in shock to face him.

'Never?'

'Never,' he confirms, and we laugh at this repetition. 'Sure, I've loved friends, family, and music, but of all the women I've dated, none were able to make me fall in love with them. I know it's not their fault. They were all kind women, but I didn't feel like opening myself enough to love anyone. But now, my heart has fallen totally, completely, and absolutely in love.' My heart warms up at this, and I feel light with happiness. 'And if this is what love feels like, then I want to be here forever,' he completes.

4 DAYS TO CHRISTMAS

21 December 2008

'Vaclavske nain or Václavské náměstí is the main square and the centre of business and culture in the New Town of Prague. It has the heaviest pedestrian traffic in the country. It's popularly called Wenceslas square and is named after Saint Wenceslas, the patron saint of Bohemia.'

The tour guide rambles on, and I listen happily to him. It's the eleventh day of the trip, and I'm sad that it will soon come to an end. Today, we're visiting Václavské nain. I had to physically drag Jace out of bed as he concluded he would rather sleep in than visit any site today, and damn if I agree to that.

Breakfast is a hilarious affair as I watch him down a big cup of coffee. Once we're full, we finally make our way to the city plaza, which is famous for being the centre of everything.

'You look radiant,' Jace says beside me, and I know I'm smiling like a fool right now.

It feels so good to be away from all that ghost drama, even if it's just for now.

Chapter Seven
Yasmine Belmont

The sun feels refreshing today, and I think it's just relief I'm feeling; relief at being in a bright, happy place, different from the past few days, which seemed to be filled with terror. Jace looks outstanding today. It could be a result of the full grin on his face, or it could be because of the way he's looking at me now.

'Why are you looking at me like that?' he asks with a sneaky smile, and I gasp.

'Look at you! You've practically been eating me with your eyes,' I exclaim with mock anger.

'Well,' he shrugs, 'you're not lying. I do want to eat you up.'

A figure brushes past us, quite rudely, if I may add, and I turn to see an older woman glaring daggers at us.

'What did I do?' I ask Jace in a quiet tone. He's about to reply when the woman strolling starts murmuring lowly.

I overheard her saying something like, 'blasted young people. Talking so brazenly about sex.'

I turn to Jace to see him trying his hardest to hold back his laughter.

'Well, she is right.' He moves to stand behind me as the woman gets further away. 'we're talking brazenly about sex.'

'How are you so nonchalant about it?' I moan. 'I feel so embarrassed.'

My cheeks feel as hot as hell.

'Because it's her opinion. That doesn't mean we have to live by it,' Jace says as he wraps his hand around my middle and then laughs into my beanie. 'You get embarrassed so easily. It's hilarious to see.'

I push his midriff slightly with the back of my elbow, 'stop making fun of me.'

'I will, princess,' he kisses my clothed shoulder.

'Let's go somewhere else.'

The street is choked up with people. As we move with the crowd, our eyes constantly look at the shops and note the things sold. Practically everything is abundant. We spend a few hours window shopping with an occasional buy. By late noon, we head to a restaurant for lunch and then head back onto the streets.

'Why don't we take a stroll around town? When we're tired, we can get a cab back to the hotel,' Jace suggests, and I wholeheartedly agree.

The stroll takes longer than we estimated, mainly because there is so much to see and do. By the time we decide to get a cab to take us back to the hotel, the sun is setting. We find a restaurant to stop by for dinner before going to the hotel.

'I'm going to change into something comfortable,' I announce as we close the door behind us.

'Go on ahead. I'll do the same,' he replies absentmindedly.

When we're done, I flop onto the bed and sprawl tiredly.

'Today was an uneventful day,' I grin.

'I love uneventful days,' Jace replies with a chuckle.

'Yeah, if only all days were uneventful.'

We go quiet after this. Each one of us seems lost in our thoughts. I decide to speak first.

'Erm, do you think we made a good decision by not agreeing to what Agatha said?'

He ponders for a short moment, 'I've been thinking about that. It was so dangerous that I didn't even wait to consider it.'

Nodding, I reply, 'yes, you're right, but we can do it and be done with it once and for all. Constantly looking over our shoulders the way we are is tiring me out and ruining our trip.'

'The problem is that we don't know the extent of their strength, and we don't actually know what they want to do with us,' he replies.

Silence resumes again, and then I exhale tiredly, 'so what do you suggest we do then?'

'Let's sleep on it. Tomorrow, we'll make a decision so we can stop taking so much of Agatha's time,' he concludes.

We get under the covers, and I lie down with my back to his front. He wraps his hand around me.

'What secret do you have to tell me?' he asks quietly.

I giggle at a fond memory. 'well, this isn't something sad or scary. It's more of a funny story, which I'll admit we need at a time like this.'

I feel his chest rumble, 'Yes. You've got that right.'

'Okay, so when I was younger, like six or seven years old, I was weirdly drawn to the evil characters in movies. When all my friends wanted to be Cinderella, I wanted to be the evil stepmother.' He barks out a laugh at this. 'When everyone wanted to be Snow White, I very much preferred the evil queen, but I kept it to myself because even then, I knew that wasn't someone I should want to emulate. When we first moved to Paris, my mum decided we should still observe Halloween. It's not common in France, but she didn't want to upset my life more by taking away the holidays I was used to. I was given free rein for my costume, and I, of course, chose something out of the ordinary. I chose Ursula, Ariel's arch-enemy, in the little mermaid.' This time, when Jace laughs again, I join in. 'My mum thought I was pranking her when I told her I wanted to be Ursula for Halloween, but when she later realised that I was being serious, she summed it up as me honouring Ariel. I don't know how she came to such a conclusion, but I knew that I would be allowed to be Ursula. Of course, I didn't dress like an evil character for Halloween after then, but if I had my way, I would have dressed as Dracula for the next Halloween.'

'You were a problematic child,' he comments at the end of my story.

'Oh, stop it. I was just a child,' I laugh. 'So, what's yours?' I ask when the laughter has died down. His face darkens immediately.

He starts by saying, 'Mine isn't as light-hearted as yours. The day before my parents died, something happened.'

He stops speaking for a long while, and I rub his hand that's on my stomach to encourage him. I can feel that this is very difficult for him to discuss.

'I wanted to go out with my friends. We were young then, and it was already late. My parents had, of course, said no, and I was visibly upset. I threw a big tantrum, and they asked me to go up to my room and not come down until the next day. As I stormed up the stairs, I remember saying to them, "I hate you, and I hope I never see you two again." Pearl was standing at the top of the stairs, and she gasped. The next morning, they went out early, and as I was still grounded, I wasn't allowed to come down.' I hear him sniff, and I turn in his arms to see tears clouding his eyes. 'And just as I said,' he said brokenly as a single tear slid down, 'I never saw them again as they died that day.'

I move and envelop him in an embrace, tucking my face in the crook of his shoulder.

'It's not your fault, baby,' I whisper.

'Yes, I know, but I can't believe that it was my last

interaction with them,' he replies, and I hug him tighter.

'But you know they would never blame you for that, right?' I ask.

'Yes,' he smiles wearily, 'they were pretty amazing people and loved us dearly. They weren't perfect, but they tried to be the perfect parents.'

We lay snuggled up against each other until we fall asleep.

3 DAYS TO CHRISTMAS

22 DECEMBER 2008

A voice breaks through my sleepy state, 'Wake up, Sleeping Beauty.'

I open my eyes to see Jace's smiling face staring down at me.

'Hold up, am I dreaming?' I ask, confused. His face scrunches up in confusion.

'You, Jace, looking so preppy this morning. Why?' I ask incoherently.

'Sorry. I don't speak jungle language,' he laughs and picks me up in his arms, making me squeal.

'You hate mornings and are typically grumpy every

morning. What's going on today?' I ask when he finally puts me down.

'Check the time,' he says simply, and I turn to look at the bedside clock.

'What?!' I exclaim, 'it's 10am already.'

'Yes, princess. You were sleeping so soundly. I've had a cup of coffee already.'

I jump towards the bathroom. 'We're going to miss out on touring today,' I yell.

After my panicked morning and Jace's accompanying laughter, we shower. I dress in a green floral top, black trousers, brown boots, a brown coat, a beanie, and warm gloves before we head to eat breakfast in a comfy little nook close to the hotel that serves delicious meals.

'Don't overeat,' I suddenly say as Jace is about to order a second helping of food.

'Why?'

'Well,' I peer down at the itinerary, 'we're going to Lease Sales Outlets at the Christmas market, and from what I've heard, there's going to be a wide selection of food and drinks.'

Just as we're finishing up, our phones ring simultaneously. My screen shows that it's my mum calling.

'It's Russ,' Jace says as he brings the phone to his ear.

I pick up mine.

'Hello, Mum.'

'Hello, my sugar, my baby,' she teases, making me laugh.

'Mum, what's with all the nicknames? Do you miss me yet?'

'Of course, I miss you, my baby girl,' she replies. 'So, where are you two now?' she asks.

'We're currently in the Czech Republic,' I reply excitedly.

'Oooh, visited the ossuary yet?' She asks, sounding just as excited as I am. I'd forgotten how much she loved reading about the ossuary.

'Yes, yes! We've visited the ossuary,' I confirm, feeling giddy with excitement.

As we continue talking, I take several glances at Jace and see that he's smiling wildly. Oh, thank God. That means that Russ's call is a good one. When I end the call, he is still talking to Russ and doesn't end the call until several moments later.

'What did he say?' I ask immediately as he drops the call. He laughs and pushes his hand through his hair.

'The best news,' he says, 'Cross is doing great.' I breathe out in relief. 'He says that the treatments are now working wonders, and he's cooperating well with the workers. He has been taken out of solitary confinement and is even talking about me, saying he misses us, his brothers.'

I'm so happy to hear this because Jace desperately

wanted it to be so. Jace abruptly stands up, and I follow suit, confusedly.

'Come on, let's get started,' he says with barely concealed energy that I can't help laughing at.

We clear the bills and move out. It's a short walk to the Lease Sales Outlets at the Prague Christmas market, and we stroll towards it. When we get there, everything I had read about paled in comparison to the sight in front of me. The market was so bright it looked like a movie. Shops upon shops lined the streets, and everywhere I turned, there was a new sight to see. Buying a pamphlet from one of the stalls, I read out loud.

'The Prague Christmas market is one of the most popular Christmas markets in Europe. The magical atmosphere, nonstop shopping, delicious food, and local Christmas traditions contribute to its popularity. You can also unwind and have cups of mulled wine.'

'Sign me up for that,' Jace says when I finish reading, and I giggle as he grabs my hand and leads me through the stalls.

The Lease Sales Outlets have an assortment of everything one would need to buy for Christmas, and we take full advantage of it.

'By the end of this trip, the souvenirs we have will be more than the clothes we have.' I laugh as Jace buys yet another gift.

The shops have so much going on that we get tired after many hours and a lot of pictures.

'Let's go grab a cup of that mulled wine they wrote about,' Jace says as he grabs my hand, and we head to where the wines are sold.

We end up having more than one cup each. It tastes terrific, and as it's late afternoon, we decide to grab some dinner. There are many restaurants in the market, and we choose a cosy-looking one that doesn't disappoint. The meal choices are great, and we have our fill before heading out.

'Our next stop for today is the Bombay Bar. We'll need to get a taxi, as it's not very close to here,' Jace says as we leave the restaurant.

The taxi takes us to the Bombay Bar in another part of Prague. It's a green-painted building with "BOMBAY BAR" written at the top in bold letters. The windows and doors are painted green as well. As it's close to evening, the sign is lit up. Upon heading inside, we notice that there are more locals than tourists. The tourists stand out because we're all looking a little wide-eyed and too excited. The bar is very cosy, and it has a dancefloor, although the dancefloor is small. We sit at the bar, and I see that the drink choices are written on a large mirror behind the bar. The bartender is amiable and explains the drinks we don't know. They do have rather excellent drink choices. Hours later, and several cups down, I feel tipsy and request some water to make me feel better.

'Let's get going,' Jace says to me. Looking at my wristwatch, I see that it's almost 10pm. We hail a taxi outside which delivers us to the hotel, and we head past the security and up to our room.

'Who turned off the heating?' I say, a little irritated and surprised. The room is freezing, not much different from the outside.

Jace picks up the phone and dials the hotel staff.

'Hello.'

'Hello, sir. Good evening,' a voice replies.

'Evening,' Jace replies. 'The heating in our room seems to have been turned off. The room number is 126, and I would like it to be turned on.'

'Of course, sir. Sorry about that. I have no idea who turned it off, as every room requires heating more than anything in such weather.'

'You're right,' Jace chuckles. 'It's rather chilly.'

We try to sit on the bed when the call ends, but the sheets are freezing, so we settle for the couch. The heating is turned on, and we sit down, waiting for the room to get warm. The drinks are kicking in, and I would love nothing more than to sleep it off.

'I think the sheets are warm enough now. Why don't you take off your robe and get into bed?' Jace suggests as he goes to touch the sheets. When he leaves the couch and moves to the bed, a sudden chill, colder than the average temperature of the room, surrounds me. I rub my hands on my thighs to get some heat in them.

'Is the heater not working?' I ask.

'It is,' Jace replies as he rubs his hands together, 'everywhere is warming up nicely.'

'I don't feel any heat,' I complain, as I feel like I'm sitting on ice.

Jace turns to look at me while taking his coat off, and I see him freeze. An icy feeling settles in my stomach.

'Jace?' I call, filled with dread.

'Yasmine, come here,' he says, but he isn't looking at me. He's looking behind me, and I'm suddenly scared.

Jace slowly puts his coat back on and holds out his hand to me. I slowly and reluctantly crane my neck behind me, and just as I'm about to see what is holding his attention, a hand as cold as ice reaches out and grabs me.

'JACE!' I scream, trying to escape its clutches.

Jace grabs hold of my outstretched hand to pull me. I look behind me and see the object of my nightmare, holding on to me with dead, rotten hands. My screams get louder as my fight to free myself gets more intense. It grabs hold of my shoulder and drags me towards itself. Upon feeling the stick sticking out of its body and its horrifying smell, I start crying.

'Let go of me!' I kick it with my legs, but it doesn't seem to budge in the slightest.

Jace lets go of my hand, and as my tears blur my vision and my fight becomes erratic, I see Jace grab a low stool and hurl it at the ghost. The stool bounces off it like bouncing off a rock, but it turns abruptly to stare at Jace. I use this split second of distraction to wrestle myself from its grasp, and I grab hold of Jace. We run out the door with the ghost hot on our trails. As we attempt to close the door behind it, it stretches out its rotten hand and grabs Jace's coat. I'm pulling Jace, but the ghost is holding on tight, so Jace shrugs out of his coat. Together, we run to the lobby where the hotel security stop us. I don't know how I'm going to explain the tears streaming down my face, but Jace takes over.

'She's not feeling so great, so we'll just go out for some fresh air.' The guards nod, then open the door for us to go out. 'Come on,' he urges me, 'we're going to Agatha.'

Sniffling and wiping my tears, I question, 'aren't you freezing? Come share my coat.'

He moves close to me as I take off my coat and hang part of it on my shoulder, giving him the other part to place on his shoulder. We walk like that in silence until we get to Agatha's hotel. As we're not with our phones, we tell the security that we're here to see someone, and he takes us to the front desk, where the receptionist asks us who we're looking for and why.

'We're here to see Agatha Jacobs,' Jace announces. 'Please tell her that Jace and Yasmine are here to see her.'

The lady dials Agatha's room. As soon as the lady mentions our names, the call drops, leaving the lady confused. Agatha comes rushing down, dressed in her sleeping robe. She looks at the two of us with panicked eyes. Turning to the receptionist, she says, 'thank you, Alice. They'll be coming in with me.'

Alice nods, and Agatha leads us to her room. It's very spacious and so warm. I can feel the cold leaving my body. We take off the coat and hang it on her rack before sitting on a couch.

'Make yourself comfortable,' she instructs as she sits facing us on the bed. 'I'm sorry. It's too late, or I would have had hot tea brought up for the two of you.'

'It's okay,' I assure her, 'we're getting warm.'

'Tell me everything that happened,' she instructs, and I launch into a detailed explanation of everything that happened.

Jace puts his arm around my shoulder, and I lean into the additional heat his body is providing. Agatha looks pensive for several long minutes, and when she finally looks at us, fear is written on her entire face.

'So, what do you suggest we do now because the attacks are getting more serious? They are beginning to touch you, and I don't know what will happen next, but it doesn't look good. We need to act fast.'

'We talked about this last night, but we didn't make a decision. I don't think we have much choice now. We know that we have to act fast as it has started to get physically deadly,' Jace says.

'So, what are we going to do? Are we going to try doing it in our hotel room?' I ask.

'No. We have plans to leave the Czech Republic tomorrow, so I'd prefer we do it in the next country we stop at,' Jace replies.

'I'm sorry that we're taking too much of your time, Agatha,' I say to her. 'You should be spending Christmas with your family and loved ones, not following us through such a spooky time.'

'Oh, pish posh,' she waves her hand, 'don't you worry about that. My conscience would never let me leave you two alone in the clutches of those things.'

We sit down in companionable silence for a long while before tiredness creeps into me, and I yawn.

'Why don't you…?' Agatha starts to say.

'We should…' Jace says at the same time, and they both stop.

'Please, go first,' Jace waves her on.

Agatha clears her throat. 'Why don't you spend the night here? I don't see any logical reason why you need to get a room when we're leaving tomorrow, anyway.'

'Yes, I was just about to say that we should get a room, but thank you. Your idea makes a lot of sense,' Jace replies.

Agatha goes down to talk to the staff, and we sit down while we wait. When she comes back with fresh sheets, we arrange them, take off our hats and shoes and lie down to sleep. Agatha goes back to bed. God, I can't wait to be done with this whole debacle.

Jace Tanner

2 DAYS TO CHRISTMAS
23 December 2008

As we make our way out of the hotel, Agatha asks, 'Where are we heading to?'

We've had breakfast already, which was a hurried affair, as we need to get moving. Looking down at the itinerary, I glance through it again before looking up at both of them.

'We're going to the North train station, and it's some distance from here.'

We get a cab. Agatha is not too concerned about being seen with us. When I ask why, she says, 'it's only now that we're leaving the Czech Republic. The ghosts won't come back again for now. When we go somewhere else, and it's been hours since your last encounters with them, there's a probability that they'll come back, so I'll be keeping my distance then.'

We get to the station, purchase our tickets, and wait for our train. While sitting, Yasmine moves closer to me. I grab hold of her hand and squeeze it lightly.

'I know things are going on,' I begin, 'but we're still on holiday, and I want you to know that, okay?'

'Okay,' she nods and smiles at me before saying, 'I know this place is not on our list of places to visit, but I know a little about it.'

'Really?' I ask, surprised. 'Go ahead then.' I don't know why I'm surprised. She is a walking mini map.

She begins softly, 'When it comes to Prague and Vienna, there are only two operators that link the two capitals, Czech Railways (CD) and Austrian Federal Railways (ÖBB). We're currently in the North train station, also known as Praha-Holešovice, which is currently the biggest train station here, but not for long.'

After her explanation, we sit in silence until our train arrives and board. The train leaves Praha-Holešovice in Prague and arrives at the South terminal in Vienna, the largest railway station in Vienna. The journey takes a little over four hours, and we have a taxi drop us off at our hotels. Agatha's hotel is right next to us, the closest we can find. We drop off our bags before moving back to Agatha's room.

'Please sit down,' she says after we enter the room.

We settle down around her, and she seems to think for some time before speaking.

'We need to do it tonight,' she says, looking at both Yasmine and me to see the effect of her statement.

I turn to look at Yasmine's scared face, and I nod to her reassuringly. She gives me back a shaky nod.

'Okay,' Yasmine replies, 'we're down for that.'

'What's it going to be like?' I ask.

'When the time comes, I'll tell you exactly what needs to be done, but for now, go on ahead and enjoy your trip.'

'Yeah, we only have two days left of the holiday,' I reply, a bit morosely. I've loved spending time with Yasmine, irrespective of the condition we've found ourselves in during this trip.

We leave her hotel and head outside.

'Okay,' Yasmine claps her hands together in a show of determination, 'let's put on our sunny smiles. We're in Austria, for God's sake. We need to make the most of the opportunity.'

Smiling at her excitement, I pull her in for a kiss, right in the middle of the walkway. She blushes and lowers her eyes, and I'm struck repeatedly by her beauty. When she lifts her eyes to mine, it's to hug me. I hold her tightly and close my eyes, immersing myself in the moment.

'Where are we going to?' She asks when we pull away.

'Nowhere in particular. We're just going to enjoy all that Vienna has to offer.'

We get a cab to take us to the town centre, where I've booked a tour bus for ease of movement. When we get there, I find the Big Bus Vienna Hop-on Hop-off Tour, show our tickets and get on. The bus fills up quickly, so the tour begins. The tour guide, a young man, points out parts of Vienna at the front of the bus as we're moving.

'First,' he begins, 'we're going to drive through Hallstatt where the timeless movie, The Sound of Music, was filmed. The Sound of Music fans will love this trip to the UNESCO-listed Salzkammergut region. You are making the most of a short stay in Austria by seeing many places in one day using our tour bus.'

He gives us a guided tour of Hallstatt and talks about its history and culture. I loved watching the movie as a child, and I'm sure that if I watched it now, the feelings would still be the same. I look over at Yasmine to see her taking picture after picture with the camera that's hung around her neck.

'Look, Jace,' she whispers excitedly, 'do you remember this spot in the movie?'

I look towards where she's pointing to see what I

remember as one of the fields that sister Maria danced in. We continue to take note of the many places as the bus drives us back to the hub of the town.

'Now,' the tour guide says, 'we're going to visit one of the most popular tourist destinations in Austria, the Schönbrunn Palace.'

A majestic, imposing structure comes into sight, and it seems like everyone on the bus has the same thought as cameras click away. The monumental building is painted yellow. The bus stops so we can get off and explore.

'Schönbrunn Palace,' he says, 'was the main summer residence of the Habsburg rulers, the imperial family. The Habsburg rulers refer to the House of Habsburgs, also called the House of Austria. It was a German dynasty that held the position of the most prominent royal house in the 11th to 20th century. It's widely regarded as one of Europe's most impressive Baroque palace structures.' We move around the palace as the tour guide continues, 'It came to be since the land was owned by the Habsburgs since 1569. The palace and garden complex were built in 1696, after the Turkish occupation, and was revamped from the ground up after 1743. There are countless chambers here that the Habsburgs resided in for most of the year. Many famous people were born here or lived here. Emperor Franz Joseph, who reigned from the mid-1800s until the second year of the first world war and married the enchanting Sisi, was born here in 1830. The monarch spent his last years of life in the palace, after which the Habsburg family fell. This building became the property of the new Republic of Austria only two years after his death. The palace became a part of UNESCO's cultural heritage because of the historical importance it has and its unique grounds and splendid holdings. The Schönbrunn Palace was opened in 1700 and has been a tourist site since the 1950s. It was named a UNESCO World Heritage Site in 1996 and is visited by an estimated eight million visitors per year. The architects were Johann Bernhard Fischer von Erlach and Nicolo Pacassi.' We move to the rooms, and the tour guide explains each ornamentation to us. 'A large percentage of these rooms are decorated in Rococo style. Some walls and ceilings are covered with white painted ornamentation covered with gold leaves.'

There are Bohemian chandeliers in many parts of the building, and the rooms vary significantly in what he described as Emperor Francis Joseph's quarters. Offices are simple, designed rooms but contrastingly, what he says are the staterooms are more lavish and fancier. There's a room called the Hall of Mirrors, and he tells us that in 1772, Wolfgang Amadeus Mozart, who was six years of age, gave a concert in the Hall of Mirrors.

'And,' he adds dramatically, 'this is the Blue Chinese Salon where, in 1918, the then Emperor Charles I abdicated the crown, marking the end of 640 years of the Habsburg's rule.'

The tour of the grounds shows that what is popularly known as Empress Sisi's former summer residence contains an enchanting park, the Palm House, the Gloriette, and a zoo. It takes a very long time to go through the palace and its grounds, and by the time we're done, we're starving. Yasmine looks hungrier than I do, though. Ugh, the relationship between women and food is not to be joked with. We head out to eat at one of the hundreds of restaurants lining the street. When we're done with our meal, we decide to head back to Agatha as the evening is approaching.

'Do we have enough time to walk back?' Yasmine asks.

I check my wristwatch and decide that it wouldn't hurt to stroll a little. If it gets too late, we can call a cab. We end up walking all the way to Agatha's hotel, where she meets us in the lobby, and we head up to her room. Yasmine sits on the couch, fiddling nervously with her hands. I stand beside her while Agatha looks on from her position on the bed.

'I have been trying endlessly to summon these ghosts, but they have adamantly ignored me and can only be found around you two,' Agatha explains.

'But we don't call them, neither do we know how to summon them. They only come as they wish,' Yasmine says despondently. She looks so tired of the situation.

Agatha smiles impishly, 'oh, but I know how you can summon them.'

'Really?' I add surprisedly.

'Yes,' Agatha confirms, 'you'll do exactly what I do when I try to summon them. The only difference will be that they will listen as you are the ones they want.' Yasmine's hands grip tightly onto mine, and I can sense her fear through her firm grip. 'All we need to do is to stay here. When it's midnight, we'll do what needs to be done so that you can be free,' Agatha instructs.

We all turn to look at the time and see it's only 8.30pm. We have a long way to go before midnight.

'Why don't you get some sleep for now?' I say to a frightened-looking Yasmine.

'You two can take the bed,' Agatha points towards the bed. 'I'm not sleeping. I'll just sit out on the balcony, and I'll wake you up when it's time.'

Yasmine and I climb into the bed, pulling the cover over our legs. When Agatha sits down on a balcony, it's hard to see her. She closes the balcony doors, leaving us alone in the room.

'You know,' Yasmine begins, 'there's something I've been doing, but not a soul knows about it.' I'm curious, so I keep quiet to encourage her to continue. 'I... I...' she seems to choke up.

I rub her shoulder. 'You can tell me, princess.'

'I've been talking to my dad for months now,' she rushes out, and I feel her body tense up in fear.

'Your mum doesn't know?' I ask, and she shakes her head.

'No, she doesn't know. I didn't mean to, but my mum has always said that I can talk to him when I want. We were just scared that he was going to hurt us, so we wanted nothing to do with him, but he somehow got my number months ago. Jace, when I heard his voice, I cried so badly. I missed him so much, and he has missed me too.'

'If your mum said that it's okay for you to talk to him when you want, why haven't you told her?' I ask.

'She feels that we have to hide from him, that he might hurt us if he finds us,' she replies in a quiet tone.

'But will he?' I ask again.

'No, he won't,' she says. 'he is sober. He has been sober for years now and has a job. He said he wants to make up for the time he has lost with me. But I think I'll tell my mum when we're back from our holiday,' she concludes, and I pull her into me, hugging her tightly. We stay quiet for a while before we start talking again.

'I've been thinking about starting up the band again when Russ and Cross are okay. If they're both interested, that is,' I confess, and her head shoots up.

'You have?'

'Yes. I have been writing songs ever since I was in therapy. I haven't written throughout our trip, but I have a lot of songs. The problem is that Aiden's gap will be felt, and I don't know how we will deal with that,' I explain, and she hugs me, whispering words of encouragement until she falls asleep.

I find myself unable to sleep. Running my fingers through her hair, I just lay there thinking until Agatha comes in and nods at me. The time is 11.50pm. It's time.

'Wake up, princess,' I nudge her. She wakes up immediately, and we climb down the bed to await Agatha's instructions.

'Okay, we're going to do this in the centre of the room, where there's enough space. I'll tell you what to do, after which I'll hide behind the balcony, so they don't see me and disappear,' she instructs, but something comes to my mind.

'Can't they just vanish when they see you?'

'No,' she replies, 'once I start the spell, they'll be stuck here until I can send them back to their world.'

'Okay then. Let's start.'

She brings out a bag from the bedside drawer and pulls out a tiny tied bag from it. She unties the little bag to reveal a white powdery substance. Shooing us back from the centre of the room, she spreads the substance in a large circle, leaving a little pile of it right in the centre. She then hands us a book with what looks like Latin written in it.

'You'll read this line,' she points to a line on the right side of the book. 'It doesn't matter if you pronounce the words perfectly. Just ensure that you pronounce it as well as you can. As long as you say each word, it'll work. Say it three times, and the ghosts will appear.'

'When do you move in?' I ask.

'As soon as they appear, I'll start reciting the binding and vanquishing spell,' she replies.

'Okay,' we reply.

Looking at the time, it's 11.59pm, so Agatha quickly runs out of the room to the balcony, where anyone or anything inside the room can't see. Yasmine looks up at me with terrified eyes. I squeeze her hands before letting go and focus on the words. Immediately, the clock strikes midnight. We recite the words to the best of our abilities. As Agatha instructed, we say it a first time, a second time, and then a third time. Nothing happens.

'Did it not...?' Yasmine says but cuts off with a scream as a hand latches onto her hand and drags her.

I'm restricted from helping her as the other ghost pulls me forward by the arm, too. Then suddenly, they both freeze as quickly as they both appeared. Their empty, dead eyes stare at us but don't see us, and their grips go lax, giving us ample opportunity to free ourselves. Agatha comes in through the balcony, reciting some words that we can't hear, but the words are enough to immobilise the ghosts.

'Get back,' Agatha throws at us, and we move back.

Taking out the small bag from a bag on her waist, she sprinkles some more powdery substance in the circle. She begins to recite a new spell, loud enough for us to hear. Although we can't understand the words, we can feel the power that resonates in the room. The air seems to stand still, and goosebumps pepper our flesh. Agatha seems lost in concentration, and her eyes take on an unearthly glow. The ghosts still stand transfixed in their spots, but wait, am I seeing things? Yasmine scoots over to me and I wrap my hand around her. No, it's real. The ghosts are vanishing, one part at a time. The legs are the first to go, followed by the midriff, and the head goes lamest. It isn't long until the circle formed by the white powdery substance is bare. I feel rather than see Agatha return to reality. The air around us moves, and the room feels normal. It's not charged with negative energy. Agatha slowly turns to stare at us, and we look worriedly at her bare expression. Her lips start stretching in a smile, and relief clouds my eyes.

'It's done,' Agatha announces triumphantly.

Yasmine Belmont

1 DAY TO CHRISTMAS
24 December 2008

'Are you leaving today?' I ask Agatha, as we all sit at the breakfast table.

The joy in the air is infectious, and one can barely stay two minutes without grinning.

'Yes, I'll leave this evening. I'm taking the night train,' Agatha replies as she bites into a piece of bacon.

'We're so thankful for all you've done for us,' Jace replies, and I turn with a smile to stare at him.

Something is off about him, though. I could feel it the moment we finally went to bed after Agatha sent away the ghosts. He looked contemplative, and I swear I saw regret flash on his face for a second, making me think it was a trick of the light. Well, whatever it is, I'm sure that he will tell me.

'Well, we have to head to Switzerland today, but we only have one place planned. The train ride is at 9am,' Jace announces.

'Why doesn't she come along, you know, so she gets to see another country? And besides, it's closer to Belgium anyway,' I suggest.

Nods of agreement follow, and we finish up our meals

before heading out to pack our bags.

Agatha meets us outside our hotel, and we get a cab together, which takes us to the train station. The train station is the same as the one we came in through, the Praha-Holešovice. We're shown our seats and buy some snacks, which we nibble on as the train progresses. After a couple of hours, when we get to the outskirts of Switzerland, we switch trains at the Zürich Hauptbahnhof, then make a final stop at Zürich Stadelhofen station. When we alight, we get a cab that drives us to our hotel. According to the taxi driver, the drive will take more than an hour, so we know we're making good time. Agatha goes on her outing, and we refresh ourselves and head out.

'Can you guess where we're going?' Jace asks with a soft smile.

'Erm,' I put my hand on my jaw in mock thought, 'Titlis?'

'You little,' he laughs, 'you saw it on the itinerary.'

I definitely did, and I'm so excited about it. We get a cab that takes us to Engelberg, the town closest to Titlis. From there, Titlis is easy to navigate. We get there to see that it's barely populated, which makes sense as it's Christmas Eve. Most people are cooped up at home cooking and watching Christmas shows or movies. A tour guide is available, and he leads us through the mountain, explaining things to us on the way.

'Titlis is a mountain located around Bern in Switzerland. It's in a mountain range located in Central Switzerland. Some parts of the western Alps are called the Uri Alps. It's popularly known as the location to first have a cable car. Its first ascent was in 1739.'

He leads us to the cable car and shows us how to strap ourselves in. Thick snow covers the mountain, giving it a white, majestic look. The ride takes a long time, and by the time we're done, I'm sure that Jace's camera is full of the number of pictures we've taken. We head out of Titlis and back to Engelberg, where we have dinner before going back to the hotel. I want to do some strolling around, but Jace is hurrying us back to the hotel. He's acting strange, but I don't want to read meaning into his actions, so I let it slide.

'I know it's only 8pm, but I think we should go to bed now,' he tells me as we close the door behind us.

My forehead wrinkles now. 'I don't understand. Go to bed by 8pm? Do we have any plans early tomorrow morning?'

'No, we don't.' He shakes his head. 'I'm just tired and need to sleep early.'

Oh, I understand. The previous day's activities have indeed been taxing. I wear my nightclothes and get under the covers, expecting him to join me. I look to see him still standing at the foot of the bed, patting his pockets.

I sit up. 'Did you lose something?'

'Yes, I can't find the itinerary.'

'Isn't it in your coat?' I ask drowsily. The bed is so warm in direct contrast to the cold environment. It's lulling me to sleep.

'No, it's not in my coat,' he replies. 'Wait, let me check reception. Maybe I left it there.' He puts his coat back on and opens the door. 'Just rest. I'll be back soon,' he smiles softly at me before closing the door behind him.

I feel like something is amiss, but I brush it off as my reliving yesterday's events, still trying to stay awake. Sleep comes hard at me, and I soon doze off. I feel a hand on my feet in my sleepy state. I ignore it. It's only when the grip becomes tighter, painful almost, that I open my eyes.

'Jace, you're hurt... Argh!' I scream as my body is thrown off the bed, tossing me to the ground.

I'm wide awake now and filled with fearful adrenaline. I scamper on my hands and knees to the other side of the wall, closer to the door, before looking back at what is attacking me. A gasp catches in my throat when I see the ghost of my nightmares, standing, staring at me. Although its face is half-rotten, I see vestiges of a smile on its lips. What is it doing here? I thought Agatha sent them back to their abyss yesterday. Could I be dreaming? Did it not work? What's going on? Where's Jace? My mind is running a mile a minute. I stand up and attempt to open the door.

To my relief, it opens, but a gnarled hand behind me reaches to slam it closed, and tears fill up my eyes.

'No! Help! Jace! Agatha!' I scream as loud as I can. My throat feels sore, and my body vibrates with fear, but I know I can't stop shouting. Someone has to hear me. Someone has to help me. I remember that Agatha's room is just a few doors down, and I scream louder. 'Someone help.'

I want to get out of here. I don't want to die. The ghost advances faster towards me, and I duck to another part of the room whenever it gets too close. Soon, I've got myself stuck in the room's corner from where there's no escape. My eyes bulge, knowing that this thing might kill me.

'Somebody help!' I scream just as the door slams open, and in runs Jace with Agatha on his heels.

Agatha is already reciting her quiet spell, and the ghost immediately gets stuck. Jace runs to me and scoops me up in his arms, which I gratefully fall into, crying at the top of my lungs. When Agatha has made the ghost vanish once again, Jace croons, 'it's okay, Princess. Agatha has sent it away.'

'No,' I scream, 'it's not okay. If it was, then how did it come back to attack me after Agatha sent it away yesterday?'

'It worked,' Agatha yells angrily. 'It worked,' she adds more calmly. 'I sent it away,' she explains at my confused expression. 'Someone summoned them again.'

The shock takes over my features as I turn to Jace to move closer to him. The guilty expression on his face makes me move back and hit my leg on the bed. No, it can't be.

'I'm sorry, Yasmine,' he whispers, with his head bent.

'Why are you apologising, Jace?' I ask in disbelief.

'I've messed up, princess. I wanted to talk to Aiden, but unknowingly, I almost got you killed.'

I look at Agatha because I don't believe this. How would Jace know how to summon a ghost?

Agatha must have seen my baffled face because she replies, 'He tore a page out of my book yesterday,' she says. 'This evening, when I was looking through my book whilst waiting for my train, I saw a page had been torn out. Coincidentally, it was the page with instructions on how to summon a ghost. I immediately knew it would be one of you, so I ran out of the station and back to the hotel. I arrived just in time to see Jace leave the hotel. As I was with my luggage, I had to come into the lobby, where the front desk officer recognised me and agreed to watch over it for me. Before I could get to where Jace was, I saw a surprised Jace talking to two ghosts. They weren't talking to him, but his voice finally rose when one of the ghosts disappeared. I heard him say, "I'm summoning Aiden, my friend, not you," and that's when I knew what had occurred.' She turns to Jace. 'When you tried to summon your friend, you didn't realise that the spell was reserved for evil ghosts. Your friend is a pure ghost and is resting in peace. So, those who had been sent back saw the opportunity and used it to come back.'

'Yasmine, I'm sorry,' Jace holds onto my hand, and I stare at him in shock.

'It's when that one ghost disappeared that we had a feeling it had come for you, so I quickly sent back the other one, and we rushed here,' Agatha completes.

Leaving a bewildered Jace and Agatha behind, I climb into bed, pull the covers over myself, and lay down. After standing there for a while, Agatha leaves to get a room, and Jace sits down on the couch with his head in his hands. I fall asleep, not allowing myself to think about it.

Jace Tanner

CHRISTMAS DAY
25 December 2008

I say to Yasmine, 'We're using the Zürich Stadelhofen station to go back to France.'

But she replies the same way she has since yesterday;

with icy silence. After we dropped Agatha off at her train this morning, where Yasmine hugged Agatha tightly and told her bye, I hadn't heard her utter a word. All my apologies have gone unanswered, so I decide to give her some space, maybe for a few hours. We're going back to France today. The cab we're in takes us to Zürich Stadelhofen station. From there, we're taken to the Zurich Hauptbahnhof. This takes us directly to France, where it stops at Gare du Nord. We take another train down to Lilli-Flanders station in Lille, where Nord, our final tourist site, is located. The train ride is tense, The train stops, and she is the first to descend. The tour guide meets us there, and although neither of us are very interested in the tour, there's nothing to lose as it's our last stop. The tour guide starts to explain, and we follow him silently with no usual excitement present.

'Nord, one of the country's most populous departments, contains the metropolitan city of Lille. Lille is the major city and one of the largest urban areas in France. The areas are larger than in Paris, Lyon, and Marseille. Nord is a department in France, and it shares a border with Belgium. Lille, the principal city of Nord, is a city that was seen as just an industrial metropolis, but not anymore. Its architecture is superb as well as its ease of life. It's a convenience of a well-known commercial city, but it's now one of France's largest metropolitan areas.'

We stroll through the city's streets, and the tour guide points to the displays of heritage buildings and some museums, galleries, hotels, and restaurants. We would explore more, but we don't have the will to do so. The streets are paved with stones; the buildings are a mixture of brown-and-red brick facades and there are golden sandstone buildings. He shows us the outer part of the Palais des Beaux-Arts, which looks great even from the outside.

He explains, 'The museum is filled with works by Goya, Rembrandt, and Rubens and is widely regarded as one of France's largest art collections.'

The tour ends, and Yasmine thanks the tour guide before we leave.

'I want to go home,' she says. Although I'm relieved that she has said something to me, this is not what I want to hear.

'Yasmine, please just hear me out,' I beg, but I see tears swim to her eyes.

'Do you really want to do this here?' she asks, and I shake my head.

'Can I come with you? So we can talk about this in private,' I ask with my heart in my throat, but she just keeps quiet. I'm going to take that as a yes.

We get a cab back to Lilli-Flanders station, which takes us to Gare du Nord. From there to her house only takes a few minutes by cab. Her mum, who had been expecting us, holds the door open and pulls Yasmine into a big hug.

'Merry Christmas, honey. I missed you so much,' she says, and Yasmine finally smiles.

'Merry Christmas to you too, Mum. I really missed you.'

Her mum hugs me as well, and I wish her a merry Christmas.

'Come in out of the cold,' her mum urges, and we rush into the warmth of the house.

'Your bags are mighty big,' she notices, and we all laugh.

'Erm, Mum, can you excuse us for a short while? We'll be in my room,' Yasmine excuses her mum, who looks at us worriedly. We head to her room and lock the door securely before she sits back on the bed.

'Jace,' she whispers, 'you almost got me killed.'

I lower myself to the chair and look at her. Pain and regret nudge at my heart.

'Princess, I know. I'm sorry,' I whisper, as I can't seem to find my voice.

'What if you and Agatha came a minute later? Why didn't you think of my safety before doing this? Or yours?'

Tears are streaming steadily down her face, and my heart pumps in fear.

'I never th… I mean… I didn't think… Yasmine, I'm

sorry. I wasn't thinking straight. I remember thinking that I had a chance to speak to Aiden and find out how he's doing over there, but I didn't think those ghosts would show up.'

She is crying softly and isn't even looking at me. I take hold of her hand; glad she hasn't pushed me away.

'Please, Princess, forgive me. I wasn't thinking straight, please.'

She turns to look at me, and as I prepare to beg again, she launches herself into my arms. I hug her tightly, so tightly I think I might hurt her. The only sound that can be heard in the room is her sniffles and my mutter, 'thank you, God, thank you, God.'

26 October 2009

'How do I look?' Russ turns to us and asks.

'Like a chick,' Cross replies tauntingly.

Russ launches himself at Cross and attempts to smack him.

'Come on, Jace. Be our referee,' Russ calls from his position under Cross's armpits.

'No way,' I shake my head. 'I'm not getting my outfit rumpled for you.'

'Aw, come on, man. Get me out of here. His armpits

stink,' Russ cries, and Cross retaliates by rubbing his armpit on Russ's face.

I look around me, my heart feeling full at the sight in front of me; everyone in the room bursts out in laughter. Russ is dressed, looking healthy and radiant. Cross is looking the best he has ever looked, as he's been clean of drugs for a long time now. Pearl smiles at their debacle while twisting her engagement ring around her middle finger. Yes, she got engaged to her girlfriend. I'm the happiest I've been in a long, long time. Well, except for one thing. Someone is missing.

'Pearl, is Yasm...?' I'm cut off by a head peeping through the door.

'Hi, everyone.'

It's her. My Yasmine. She is dressed to perfection. She's in her emerald green dress that stops mid-thigh, and clings to her body, with a pair of strappy shoes and earrings and bangles that I bought for her in Germany.

A chorus of 'Hi, Yasmine,' rings throughout the room.

She hugs everyone, starting with Russ, then Cross, Pearl and finally me.

'Saving the best for last, I see,' I tease.

'As I should,' she says as I kiss her.

She is doing great at her master's program, and I'm so proud of her. Shouts of approval from the inhabitants of the room make her blush.

'Alright, we'll be outside,' I lead Yasmine outside.

We head to a bench in the hallway, and we sit. I pull her into my body and hold her tight.

'I have a secret to tell you,' I say.

'You do?' she says, surprised. Since the trip, we haven't done this, and I know I've surprised her.

'I know I told you and everyone else that I wanted to start our band again. But I only thought that we'd mainly do small shows, if any shows at all. This is not what I expected. We're about to perform in one of the biggest concert halls in America. Thousands of people bought our music, listened to it and are here for our show. Our two albums have been nominated for the album of the year, and we're one of the most popular bands in the world. Princess, I didn't expect this. This level of success for a three-legged band is hard to come to terms with.'

That is what we've been jokingly calling ourselves: a three-legged band. We were a full table, and we've lost one leg of the table. It's an inside joke.

'Let me tell you something,' Yasmine replies. 'You may not have expected your fame to come back this fast, but it did. You're the most humble, genuine man I've ever met, and you love your bandmates like they are your blood. Your music is great, and your personality is incredible. It's a given that you'll go far. Besides, Aiden's spirit is with you.'

Aiden's spirit; it's with me. I turn to her and kiss her. Not a shallow kiss meant for others to see, but a deep one that reflects my love and devotion toward her.

'Get a room,' a crew member shouts, and laughter follows. Flipping them off, I pull a smiling Yasmine to her feet.

'Where are we heading to?' she asks.

'To get a room,' I reply slyly.

'No!' she says with a laugh.

'Okay then. Let me kiss you the way I want right here.'

She squeals and drags me into the room I was heading in. It's another dressing room, but this one is thankfully empty. Putting my hand on her waist, I lift her onto a counter-like surface. Her dress rides up, and I step in between her legs, kissing her deeply. Her lips part under mine, the way they always do, and the sweetness of her mouth makes me yearn for her touch and the heat of her body. My hands move to her face, where I angle her face the way I want. The feel of her soft body pressed against mine is intoxicating in the way few things are, and my hands creep to her soft breasts, palming them over her dress. She pulls away, blushing hard as she looks at the door, which could be barged into at any minute because I didn't lock it.

'We can stop now,' I say as I try to get my breathing under control. The sight of her eyes, darkening with need, makes it so difficult to pull away. I finally pull away and lift her down from the dresser, helping her straighten her clothes and hair. She just looks at me with that small adoring smile of hers.

'Oh,' she looks in her purse and pulls out a piece of paper, 'my mum sent this to you.'

She has moved from Paris, and we live together here in America, but she visits there frequently. The paper reads,

Hey Jace, I know this is your biggest show yet, and you might be feeling nervous. Well, I just wanted to remind you that my daughter thinks you are her moon and star, and you've proven times without number that you think even more highly of her. Let this knowledge of your support team fuel you to do great. Your sister loves you; your brothers love you; my daughter loves you, and I love you. You're going to do great.

It's this note, the face of my sister and Yasmine, the woman I love, that stays in my mind as we walk into the arena to deafening shouts of 'Soft Division! Soft Division!'

Yes. I, Jace on the right, Cross to my left, and Aiden watching above us are Soft Division. We start with our most famous song, and it's also our favourite song, "Aiden's home."

Yes, we're Soft Division.

Reviews are the most powerful tools for a publisher and an author, they help to gain attention for the books you enjoy reading. Honest reviews of our books help to bring them to the attention of other readers.

If you have enjoyed this book or any of our other books we would be very grateful if you could spend just five minutes leaving a review. These reviews can be as short or as long as you like.

www.ingramcontent.com/pod-product-compliance
Lightning Source LLC
Chambersburg PA
CBHW022103150426
43195CB00008B/253